D0076365

FIELD
CASEWORK

ENTREPRENEURSHIP AND
THE MANAGEMENT OF GROWING ENTERPRISES

A Sage Publications Series

Series Editor	Jerome A. Katz
	Saint Louis University
	Jefferson Smurfit Center for Enterpreneurial Studies
Advisory Board	D. Ray Bagby, *Baylor University*
	Donald F. Kuratko, *Ball State University*
	Justin Longnecker, *Baylor University*
	Ian C. MacMillan, *University of Pennsylvania*
	Howard H. Stevenson, *Harvard University*
	Frederick C. Scherr, *West Virginia University*
	Jeffry A. Timmons, *Babson College*

FIELD
CASEWORK
Methods for Consulting to Small and Startup Businesses

LISA K. GUNDRY
AARON A. BUCHKO

EMGE

SAGE Publications
International Educational and Professional Publisher
Thousand Oaks   London   New Delhi

Copyright © 1996 by Sage Publications, Inc.

All rights reserved. No part of this book may be reproduced or utilized in any form or by any means, electronic or mechanical, including photocopying, recording, or by any information storage and retrieval system, without permission in writing from the publisher.

For information address:

SAGE Publications, Inc.
2455 Teller Road
Thousand Oaks, California 91320
E-mail: order@sagepub.com

SAGE Publications Ltd.
6 Bonhill Street
London EC2A 4PU
United Kingdom

SAGE Publications India Pvt. Ltd.
M-32 Market
Greater Kailash I
New Delhi 110 048 India

Printed in the United States of America

Library of Congress Cataloging-in-Publication Data

Gundry, Lisa K., 1958-
  Field casework: Methods for consulting to small and startup
  businesses / authors, Lisa K. Gundry, Aaron A. Buchko.
      p. cm. — (Entrepreneurship and the management of growing
    enterprises)
  Includes bibliographical references and index.
  ISBN 0-8039-7200-8 (cloth : acid-free paper). — ISBN 0-8039-7201-6
(pbk. : acid-free paper)
    1. Business consultants—Case studies. 2. Small business—
Management—Case studies. 3. Case method. I. Buchko, Aaron A.
II. Title. III. Series.
HD69.C6G853 1996
001—dc20   95-41765

This book is printed on acid-free paper.

96 97 98 99 10 9 8 7 6 5 4 3 2 1
Sage Production Editor: Astrid Virding

For my sons, Dylan & Austin
L.G.

For my daughter, Alex
A.B.

Contents

Series Editor's Introduction   xi
   Jerome A. Katz

Acknowledgments   xiii

Preface   xv

1. The Purpose and Goals of Fieldwork   1
   Quick Tips   1
   The Role of Fieldwork in Business Courses   2
   Fieldwork's Contribution to Higher Education   4
   Why Should I Participate in Fieldwork?   5
   The Student's Role in Fieldwork   9
   How Clients Evaluate Fieldwork   10
   The University's or College's Role in Fieldwork   12
   Embarking on Fieldwork: Things You Can Do to Prepare   13
   Ready . . . Set . . .   14
   References   15

2. The Fieldwork Experience: What It Is and What It Isn't   17
   Quick Tips   17
   What Is Appropriate Fieldwork?   18
   Some Typical Fieldwork Projects   20
   Some Common Myths About Fieldwork   21

3. Managing the Fieldwork   29
   Quick Tips   29
   The Assessment Phase   30
   Information Gathering and Preliminary Analyses   31

Initial Meetings With the Client	37
Establishing the Purpose and Scope of the Project	40
The Implementation Phase	46
Establishing Objectives	46
Developing the Action Plan and Methodology	49
Plan Execution	52
Preparing the Final Report	54
The Results Phase	56
Presentation of the Deliverables	56
Follow-Up Activities	59
Conclusion	61
References	61
4. Managing the Student Consulting Team	63
Quick Tips	63
The Nature of Student Consulting Teams	64
Group Structure and Roles	68
The Project Manager	68
The Task Managers	70
Team Members	70
Group Development and Group Dynamics	73
Group Formation	73
Group Dynamics	77
Intergroup Conflict	80
Conclusion	83
Reference	83
5. Launching the Fieldwork Information Search	85
Quick Tips	85
Primary and Secondary Sources of Information	87
Step 1: Deciding What Information Is Needed	87
Step 2: Gathering Information	89
Annotated Bibliography of Secondary Sources	89
Primary Sources of Information	90
Surveys and Questionnaires	90
Interviews	92
Step 3: Organizing the Information	94
Step 4: Interpreting the Information	95
Reference	97
6. Developing Recommendations and the Final Client Presentation	99

Quick Tips   99
Review of Information and Research   102
Generation of Alternatives   104
Evaluation of Alternatives   105
Selection of Alternatives   107
Implementation   108
   Consistency   109
   Step-by-Step Instructions   109
Conclusion   112
A Final Word   113

Appendix A: Professionalism, Confidentiality,
  and Ethical Considerations of Fieldwork   115

Appendix B: The Role of the SBA/SBI in Fieldwork   119

Appendix C: Annotated Bibliography of Secondary Sources   123
References   123
   Industry Sources   124
   Demographic Sources   124
   Entrepreneurship and Small Business Sources 124
Abstracts and Indexes   126
Book Reviews   127
Internet Sources   127
Research Methods   128
Creative Problem-Solving Sources   129
Government Agencies   129
Periodicals   133
Newsletters   134

Index   135

About the Authors   137

Series Editor's Introduction

More than ever, entrepreneurship is important. For most of the developed world it is the engine of innovation and job creation, and for the less developed world it is the path to self-sufficiency, personal freedom, and membership in the world economic community.

Entrepreneurship can't be stopped. When governments restrict it, individuals sneak off and develop their own businesses in what we call "the underground economy." While entrepreneurship can't be stopped, it *can* be helped—through the opportunities created by government, technology, trade, and individual creativity and ambition. Most important, entrepreneurship can be helped through education, training, and counseling, and therein lies the purpose of Sage Publications' series on **Entrepreneurship and the Management of Growing Enterprises**, or EMGE for short.

The traditional model for passing along written information on entrepreneurship has focused on two extremes: the classic textbooks and "trade" books, which have increasingly become very long and very general to cover the tremendous growth of information available for aspiring and growing entrepreneurs, and the pamphlet, which offers specific information in a typically very brief form. EMGE was started as a middle-ground alternative, providing top experts in entrepreneurship worldwide an opportunity to give specific, detailed, and in-depth information of the major topics and techniques in entrepreneurship.

As you read books in this series you will see certain commonalities: a focus on one topic or activity, a strong practical orientation *grounded* in the latest and most solid research in entrepreneurship, and hopefully a book that is easy-to-read and easy-to-apply.

If we achieve this, the credit will go to a large number of people. The series gains invaluable insights from an advisory board of the leaders in entrepreneurship education and research, including the authors of the top texts in entrepreneurship: Don Kuratko (Ball State), Justin Longnecker (Baylor), Jeff Timmons (Babson), and Howard Stevenson (Harvard), and the editors of the three major research journals—Ray Bagby of *Entrepreneurship: Theory and Practice,* Ian MacMillan of the *Journal of Business Venturing,* and Fred Scherr of *Journal of Small Business Management.* Our support at Sage Publications has been longstanding, long-suffering, and invaluable in its own right, including the work of Marquita Flemming, Harry Briggs, Kris Bergstad, Astrid Virding, Anne West, and Sage's visionary leader Sara Miller McCune. Most important has been the support of three key "publics": the series authors; Saint Louis University's Jefferson Smurfit Center for Entrepreneurial Studies; and most of all my family—Cheryl, Lauren, and Joshua. To all of these I express my sincerest appreciation for support and encouragement.

The next steps are up to you—either as a student of entrepreneurship, an entrepreneur, or a professional assisting or teaching entrepreneurship. EMGE remains an open-ended series and we seek manuscripts and ideas for additional volumes that detail, explore, and make real the skills and ideas central to the creation and growth of business worldwide. We also want to hear from our readers regarding the volumes themselves. I can be reached at the Jefferson Smurfit Center for Entrepreneurial Studies, Saint Louis University, 3674 Lindell Blvd., St. Louis, MO 63108, or through Sage Publications.

—Jerome A. Katz
Series Editor

Acknowledgments

This book is the culmination of much time spent immersed in field-work projects. We have managed, coached, soothed, and cheered our students (and ourselves) onward during the years we have overseen these often tumultuous yet exhilarating learning experiences. But this book is not just a medium for us to share our methods with readers. It materialized through the experiences of many others who deserve deeply felt thanks for the coaching and support they have given us.

The only place to start is with our appreciation to Jerome Katz, Series Editor of our book, and visionary and model extraordinaire among entrepreneurship educators. His ideas and insights gave rise to our thoughts and, later, written words. His belief in the value of entrepreneurship education and fieldwork kept us moving toward our goal.

Marquita Flemming, Management and Marketing Editor at Sage Publications, uplifted us with every conversation and gave us exceptional assistance and support during our writing. Several colleagues at DePaul University's College of Commerce deserve recognition: Harold Welsch, Gerhard Plaschka, Ilya Meiertal, Joe Roberts, and Jill Kickul. Colleagues in the Business Management & Administration Department of the Foster College of Business at Bradley University who have been involved with the program deserve recognition: Fred Fry, Laurence Weinzimmer, Charles Stoner, William Clarey, and Janice Stringer and the administration, as do the graduate students at Bradley who have coordinated the program along with Roger Luman and Michael Monahan of the Small Business Development Center.

We owe heartfelt thanks to the countless numbers of students, many pseudonymed in this work, and clients who have given of their time and effort to carry out fieldwork and have shared experiences with us.

Our families have contributed immeasurably to this work. Lisa's husband, Peter, keeps her infinitely supplied with inspiring "field tales," and Dylan and Austin generously and selflessly shared her with her pen and computer these many months. Aaron's wife, Kathy, and daughter, Alex, whose patience and efforts gave him the time to do the writing necessary for the book—all deserve our gratitude. •

Preface

Increasingly, colleges and universities are incorporating some type of formal course or program that requires students to apply their knowledge and education to actual business problems. Such courses are typically called "Senior Project," "Fieldwork Experience," "Business Consulting," or the like. Whatever the title, the purpose of the course is to provide students with actual "hands-on" experience in dealing with the problems and complexities of running an actual business organization.

In the "typical" fieldwork course (if there is such a thing), a team of students—generally in the advanced stages of their program of study—will be assigned to work with the owners, founders, or managers of a local business organization. The team's purpose is to provide information and advice to the client that will assist the client in improving the operations and performance of the organization. The students therefore act as consultants—those who give professional advice or services.

More and more colleges and universities are recognizing the value of such an experience as part of the students' program of study. Giving students hands-on experience allows them to gain insights and learning that is just not possible within the sterile walls of the classroom or from a textbook case. The opportunity to apply the knowledge learned through academic instruction within the relative safety and security of the university setting is an invaluable educational experience. It's rather like medical school—you can learn all about anatomy and physiology, but until you use that scalpel for the first time on a real patient you don't really understand what is involved in surgery. The fieldwork experience gives students the chance to exercise their skills and to develop new skills—in

communications, team building, project management, and other areas—
that are particularly important to future professional success.

In addition, the fieldwork experience is one that students will long
remember and one that adds to their education. We are constantly amazed
that when we meet alumni 10 or 15 years after graduation, virtually all
of them can recall their fieldwork project course, even to the point of
telling us who the client was and what the problems were that their
team addressed. (At the same time, most cannot recall anything they
learned in a specific course!) The fieldwork experience makes an impression on students.

As faculty in our respective business schools, we have had many years
of experience working with students on fieldwork projects. Because of
the size and structure of our fieldwork programs, we have had literally
thousands of students go through the program and serve hundreds of
clients. We have noticed that certain issues were constantly recurring in
the course of the project—issues such as

- What is fieldwork like?
- How does consulting work?
- How do I get information about the client or the industry?
- I need to develop a relationship with the client—what is the best way to do this?
- How do we figure out what the client wants or expects from us?
- What is a good structure for managing the process that will achieve high results while minimizing the pain?
- What do I need to include in the Final Report?
- How can I manage a diverse team of individuals to ensure that we'll all get along while going through the process?
- These and similar questions seem to be on students' minds as they prepare for their initial fieldwork project.

We have also noticed that there was very little information available
to students about how to "get through" the fieldwork experience—at
least information that was in one concise form. There were many books,
manuals, and articles that we could tell students to read, but there wasn't
a simple, brief, yet thorough treatment of the subject. So, in desperation,
we began to write up our own guidelines for students.

This monograph has grown out of our efforts to provide our students with information and guidelines to help manage the fieldwork process. It is based on our years of experience and hundreds and thousands of clients and students who have gone through our programs. As such, it represents our initial efforts to get into writing the accumulated wisdom and experience that for too long has been "handed down" from professor to student in conversations, lectures, and orientation sessions. We hope that by so doing we will provide students with a boost to their confidence as they approach what—for most of them—is a somewhat intimidating experience. If students realize that others have gone through the experience and survived (reasonably well), then they will be better equipped to do so themselves. We hope this will lead to a better educational experience and will at the same time provide increased performance and service to the client.

We recognize that, for most students, this will be their first—and often only—experience as a consultant. We also realize that having to work with "real" businesspeople and organizations with real problems and providing advice that will affect the decisions that these individuals will make regarding their businesses can be intimidating. But we also know that nothing else in the student's academic program compares with fieldwork. When done well, it is the highlight of their education; when done poorly, it is their worst nightmare. Our goal is to equip students better for a positive experience by providing a realistic preview and guidelines that have been proven to work for many students who have survived the fieldwork experience.

—Lisa K. Gundry
—Aaron A. Buchko

1 | The Purpose and Goals of Fieldwork

Quick Tips

- Field cases are holistic, have widely varying degrees of available information, a higher degree of personal contact and intervention, and the potential for a stronger future impact on decisions than textbook cases.
- By doing fieldwork, you are really learning "experientially" (through hands-on experience). As a result, you will strengthen your ability to identify problems, seek information, consider multiple perspectives, propose a set of actions, and recognize the business organization as a system of interrelated parts.
- Fieldwork integrates your academic experience with professional experience, lets you apply your business skills to teach others, and helps you to establish contacts in the business world.
- Clients generally have evaluated field cases very positively, especially when student consultants: Make sure they fully address the problem, keep the client continually informed of the project's progress, and listen effectively.
- There are places on your campus where you can seek assistance for many aspects of fieldwork.

- In preparation for fieldwork, get to know the campus library, visit the student employment center, and talk to other students who have previously completed field cases.

THE ROLE OF FIELDWORK
IN BUSINESS COURSES

Welcome to the world of fieldwork! By now you have probably spent several semesters or quarters arming yourself to the teeth with general business acumen—functional and operational business skills in accounting, management, marketing, finance, and economics. At last you have an opportunity to test your mettle and apply these skills to a real business. We use the term *real* here to connote an existing business whose members are people with whom you will interact on a regular basis. In what ways will this experience be different from any you have had before in your academic career? Many of you have had extensive experience using business cases in a textbook or other written format in a course. These often have complete information, including financial records and history of the firm. Some have in-depth characterizations of the founders, key personnel, and other stakeholders in the business. There are, however, several fundamental differences between the written case and the field-based case. Table 1.1 outlines some of the factors that contribute to very different learning outcomes.

Consider how the following students described this difference:

"One important aspect of the live case project was that I was able to actually witness the motivation that the entrepreneur had with his idea. Unlike textbook cases, where sometimes it is even difficult to imagine that an individual is part of a case because of all the concrete information, the live case allowed me to see how dedicated an entrepreneur can be, and how much effect a case can have on him." (Allen, Business Administration major)

"The fact that these were real businesses with real problems made it different than the cases we were used to doing in other manage-

Table 1.1   A Comparison of Written and Field-Based Cases

Written Cases	*Field-Based Cases*
Narrower approach; written to illustrate a few points or concepts	Holistic approach; many points or concepts related to a topic available to observe
Information is strategically manipulated; presented or withheld in line with the purpose	Information is available; some may be inaccurate or randomly distorted
Little or no personal contact with case characters	High degree of personal contact with people
Little or no intervention possible; cannot alter case facts or presentation	High degree of intervention possible; multiple perspectives can be solicited
No future impact on decisions	High future impact on decisions
No follow-up possible; case cannot "progress" unless new parts are written	Follow-up possible; each case is different in subsequent analyses

ment courses from a reading. We felt that we had some real impact on the business if we would offer help, instead of just commenting on the problems of the written cases without knowing what impact it might have on the business." (Jill, Marketing major)

"After all these years of reading and memorizing, I was finally able to put those things to use. Through not having to rely on a textbook for answers, I was able to assess myself and my abilities, something I have never been able to do from a textbook. I also learned that there is a need for what is in textbooks and the transition from the text to the real world is very meaningful." (Stephanie, Finance major)

"The real learning came from making phone calls, working on spreadsheets, designing surveys, compiling and analyzing results, and group discussion. Once I got involved with the case I found myself caring about the work we were doing. Fictitious cases and textbook problems don't supply that kind of emotion. For example, if I were working on a textbook problem and ran into an obstacle, I might be tempted to submit the problem with less than a one-hundred-percent effort. But when I am working on a real case and people's futures could very well depend on my effort, I know that I will give one-hundred percent." (Ron, Accounting major)

FIELDWORK'S CONTRIBUTION
TO HIGHER EDUCATION

Fieldwork is *experiential* in nature. A framework for this type of learning, proposed by Kolb, Lublin, Spoth, and Baker (1987), is described below and will help you understand how fieldwork can help you gain the competencies you need to become (or continue to be) an effective manager. Several learning objectives can be seen:

• *Behavioral competence:* Taking the initiative to seek information and propose a set of actions as a result of the search, all within the context of an uncertain organizational environment.

• *Perceptual competence:* Identifying the correct problem(s); gathering, organizing, and interpreting information; and considering multiple perspectives.

• *Affective competence:* Developing empathy and sensitivity to others' views, and managing disagreements constructively.

• *Symbolic competence:* Conceptualizing the business as a system of interrelated parts; considering how a change in one component affects the entire organization.

As Buller (1992) has stated, fieldwork courses place students in a real-time environment in which the people, problems, solutions, and results all have real impact. He notes that this real-life experience is visibly absent from the traditional business school curriculum.

Put simply, field consulting work can sharpen your professional skills as you

• identify a problem or opportunity faced by a business

• consider what in fact needs to be done; this involves "walking a mile in another person's shoes" (e.g., the founder, a key officer or manager, an employee, or a customer) to view the business through their eyes

• determine what information you need to learn more about the problem

• discover where to find relevant information and how to interpret the information

• strengthen your ability to function as a group member and develop a cross-disciplinary understanding of business problems

• empathize with others and respect their views, rather than argue your own turf, as you generate ideas and propose alternatives

• recognize that any organization (no matter how small) is a complex system. Any solution must recognize the relationships and effects among all the parts ("parts" include departments or other units, products and services, and, certainly, the people in the organization). Further, good solutions come with instructions to implement and to evaluate their effectiveness.

Ramocki (1987) contends that, "Profound benefits come from fieldwork projects. . . . [Among these are that] students leave the course with demonstrated higher levels of overall research abilities and self-confidence" (p. 29).

WHY SHOULD I PARTICIPATE IN FIELDWORK?

This is a valid question, and one that most students admit to asking themselves, if not their professors. After all, you probably had some choice in deciding which courses to take as part of your curriculum. You selected this one, and although you may not yet know it, you did so for any (or all) of the following reasons:

• *To integrate your education with practical experience.*
No other situation gives you quite the same opportunity to conduct an assessment of an existing business (at the request of, not as a favor granted by, the founder or manager); to immerse yourself in the business for an extended period of time (no one-shot visit is this!); to pursue alternative solutions (calling for your creativity as well as your business ingenuity); and to present the findings to your client in the hope of

having a real impact on the lives of others. As these student consultants put it,

> "This was the first time that I was actually able to use textbook knowledge and apply it to 'real' situations in the 'real' world."

> "Of all the things I have learned from this course, the most valuable have come from the live case project. The case encouraged me to use principles learned from this class and other classes; go beyond what one could learn simply from reading a textbook; and use my common sense to make important decisions to help a struggling business. It really gave me a sense of what I have learned throughout my college life."

> "What was new was the hard fact that there was someone's life work at stake. It didn't really hit me until we, as a group, paid a visit to our client. As I looked around the shop and listened to [the client] talk to us about her business, I could not believe that I was really not working out of the textbook anymore. Assessments that we made would be acknowledged by her, and if these assessments were not correct, we may be indirectly responsible. That kind of pressure is something that books do not teach, or sometimes even address."

Fieldwork affords you a professional advantage. Reality shock will not be so great when you enter full-time work after college, or start your own business down the road. Attending classes, reading textbooks and other materials, and listening to guest lecturers are definitely valuable (and necessary) parts of life in higher education. But just as your first attempt behind the steering wheel was *nothing* like you anticipated in driver's education class, the world of work is more complex and multidimensional than you expected. The more *reality-based* experiences you can collect for yourself while in college, the better prepared you will be for what lies ahead of you as a business owner, manager, or employee.

- *To position yourself at the cutting-edge of your field.*

Just as entrepreneurs must carve out and sustain a competitive position, so too should you differentiate your own career from your competition's. Only a small percentage of business students participate in fieldwork (although it predictably is increasing as the benefits become known). Imagine the number of résumés the average company receives every year from soon-to-be college graduates. Companies such as IBM receive hundreds of thousands per year, smaller firms often receive hundreds of résumés. What will catch a recruiter's eye and induce him or her to give you serious consideration? We know from many actual experiences that fieldwork completed as part of your coursework does raise the eyebrows and interest of recruiters. And we know this because of the many conversations we have with such recruiters, who notice your field consulting experience on your résumé, are intrigued, and phone or write us to learn more about your consulting project.

Rhonda, a Management major, offered this comment:

> "This experience of working with a real entrepreneur is one that few people, let alone college students, get to encounter. Not many people can say that they helped develop a successful business while they were in college."

As professors (and sometimes as your references), we are more likely to be asked about the fieldwork you mention on your résumé than about anything else that is there.

OK, so you know you are not headed to the corridors of Corporate America upon graduation. You want to start your own business. What better way to learn what to do (and not to do) than by getting inside an already existing entrepreneurship or small business? You're also likely, by the way, to get to know suppliers, customers, bankers, and entre-preneurial agencies (government and private sector) through fieldwork. As expressed by these students,

> "What the books will never be able to explain is the role that perseverance plays in any start-up endeavor. An entrepreneur spends countless hours working on perfecting his or her idea through col-lecting feedback or whatever. An entrepreneur gets denied financ-ing, help, time, everything more times than they would ever care to remember, let alone admit publicly. Books can never give anyone guts to take a chance or the heart to stick it out." (José, Finance major)

"In the textbook, the cases dealt with many entrepreneurs who were successful. The case that I worked on was not such a successful firm. Being an entrepreneur is not what I thought it would be. I imagined that all entrepreneurs were like the type you read about—the rags to riches or the overnight success stories." (Shaun, Marketing major)

- *To improve your business skills by teaching them to others.*

Say you know how to construct and interpret a P&L (Profit and Loss) statement. Great! Now teach someone who has never taken an accounting course how to do it (and do it repeatedly, quarter by quarter, year after year). Fieldwork allows you to go beyond applying your skills in a problem, by training and developing others to solve the problem. In this way you exponentially increase the value of your skills. You also quickly find out where the gaps in your learning lie and can fill them while still in college. Some students may approach the consulting cases with understandable trepidation:

"I had never done this before in all of my classes. When the professor said that we have a live case to apply what we had learned from class to the real world, I was so scared that I might goof up. I don't want the entrepreneur to go out of business because of my mistake. But after the case was done, I was so happy that I had finished it and that I really had offered advice to help the entrepreneur." (Tanya, Accounting major)

- *To establish contacts in business.*

Fieldwork puts you in touch with business people. You set your own limit as to how many you want or need to meet to complete your project. The payoff here is obvious. Networking has become much more critical in the 1990s, and pursuing contacts early (or later) in your career can only be an advantage. Fieldwork may enable you to develop a mentoring relationship with an entrepreneur who has experienced the highs and lows of business ownership and can communicate them to you. Also, there are sometimes happy endings as a student is offered a job by the fieldwork client—*after* the project has ended, of course. For more on why AFTER is so important, see Appendix A on Professionalism, Confidentiality, and Ethical Considerations of Fieldwork.

- *To work in a field you haven't considered.*

Perhaps as a finance major, you someday intend to seek work in a large corporate finance department, say a manufacturing firm's. It so happens that your fieldwork assignment is to a small retail shop, where your task is to create a more effective method of record keeping and help the owner decide if she should seek a loan for expanding to a second store. You just might discover some creative, and not previously thought of, uses for your financial know-how that you otherwise never would have uncovered. Now you have more choices than you thought you did before this project.

> "As an accounting major, I am no stranger to hard work. Unfortunately, I spent so much time concentrating on my major that all other courses took a backseat. This preoccupation kept me from seeing how the other business disciplines fit into the real world. This project, a crash course in the real world, taught me the significance of all the business disciplines and how they interrelate."

- *To consider a field in which you haven't worked.*

Not the least of the advantages of fieldwork is that you will have an opportunity to hear about other field cases in which your classmates are involved. A student was interested in working in (or someday even establishing) an art gallery in the future. Although his fieldwork assignment was to a freight transport company, he heard the in-class presentation of a project another team was working on with an arts organization. Through the *other* team's connection, he was able to meet the owner of a local gallery and talk himself into an internship for the next academic term to learn more about the business.

THE STUDENT'S ROLE IN FIELDWORK

One way to determine your role and responsibility is to begin with your final, deliverable product—the consultant's report. A much more detailed review of the Final Report's components is provided in Chapter 6. Suffice it to say here, however, that a report of quality should meet at least the following criteria:

• The report reflects the client's needs that were assessed at the start of the fieldwork and mutually agreed upon between the student(s) and the client.

• The report is well documented, written logically and cohesively, and uses language understood by the client for whose benefit it is written.

• Recommendations include options and alternative courses of actions that can be taken.

• A set of action steps is given, with time frame, personnel and other resources required, and priorities clearly outlined.

• Recommendations are feasible and implementable for the client. Any knowledge or instructions that the client needs to carry out your recommendations are provided or referred by you.

• Supporting evidence from external sources is included, with references to all works cited.

• The report is professionally presented, and criticisms are offered constructively with suggestions for remedying problems.

• The potential for making a difference in the business is clearly articulated (e.g., growth, return on investment [ROI], profitability, reducing expenses, etc.).

HOW CLIENTS EVALUATE FIELDWORK

Studies have been conducted that examine clients' and students' perceptions about fieldwork. Here are some of the results of these surveys to help you better understand what clients expect of student consultants.

Fry (1985) investigated the factors related to successful fieldwork using Small Business Institute (SBI) clients and students. Some of the most important variables related to the final project grade were: (a) length of the report text, suggesting substantial analysis, not "padding" of the report with exhibits because these were not counted in the variable "total report length"; and (b) the reaction of the student team to the client, including how well the project went and the degree of interest that students had in the project.

In a study of client satisfaction levels (Kiesner, 1987), clients reported an overall strongly positive feeling about their encounter with a student team. Of note is that one fifth of the 146 small-business owners surveyed claimed that students didn't *fully* address their problems. Kiesner advised that education is needed on both sides: Owners need to be aware that their views of the business problem may be distorted and not the whole truth; likewise, students should be sure that they are working on the real problem and are keeping their clients informed about their progress.

On four critical dimensions of evaluation—professionalism, knowledge, practicality, and overall value—Weinstein, Nicholls, and Seaton (1992) found that clients' favorable perceptions clearly outweighed unfavorable ones. Similarly, O'Connor and Rogers (1988) found that both students and clients agreed that the SBI case situation was very worthwhile. Specifically, the study revealed that clients need more information from professors and SBI directors regarding the purpose and procedures involved in SBI to alleviate concerns that could disrupt the client-student relationship. Further, clients perceived that students could be better trained with regard to communication skills, primarily the art of listening.

This leads to some action steps students can take to ensure that the fieldwork begins on a positive note.

• Ask your client to explain what he or she understands about the procedures involved in fieldwork (number of meetings to hold, paperwork to be completed, etc.). Relay any questions or misunderstandings to your instructor as soon as possible. This sets expectations appropriately and prevents misunderstandings from escalating later.

• At all client meetings, maintain eye contact and avoid burying your head in your notebook. Have one team member write while others listen, or ask if you can tape meetings so all you have to do is take very brief notes. Clarify what you don't understand: "So, you feel the primary goal of this advertising plan should be . . . " Avoid evaluative statements, such as "You don't do this correctly . . . ," that put clients on the defensive. There are many reputable and thorough sources of communications training manuals for you to consult. Ask your instructor or a librarian.

THE UNIVERSITY'S OR
COLLEGE'S ROLE IN FIELDWORK

The assignment of student consultants to local businesses to help solve problems is certainly a valuable service that educational institutions can offer to their local communities (Robichaux, 1990). In this way, the connection between the classroom and the business environment is profound and near.

Your university or college may have a Small Business Institute, sponsored by the United States Small Business Administration, that oversees fieldwork completed in entrepreneurship and small business courses. The SBI is further discussed in Appendix B as a representative form of fieldwork. The SBI provides community service by helping small businesses to receive needed assistance and provides academic service to students who desire practical application of business skills.

If your school does not have an SBI, there are other departments, institutions, or centers that can provide assistance and support to you while you are carrying out your fieldwork. Look for help and information from the following and other places on campus or the city/town in which you are located.

- Academic departments (Management, Marketing, Accounting, Finance, etc.) in the business school and other schools in the university, for specific information related to functional-level problems.

- Research institutes on campus, such as interdisciplinary centers for research on technology and business, entrepreneurial centers, and so on.

- Teaching institutes for information on adult and continuing professional education programs and services that may provide training for businesspeople.

- Alumni Relations

- Assessment Centers (for skills inventories)

- University Relations (media relations, lists of business partners, etc.)

- Legal clinic, for business law-related issues

- Libraries (much more on this in Chapter 5)

- Student Life/Student Organizations (Entrepreneurship Club, Marketing Club)

EMBARKING ON FIELDWORK:
THINGS YOU CAN DO TO PREPARE

By this time, you probably realize that fieldwork is an experience unlike any other you have had in college, so consider taking the initiative and doing some things to prepare yourself. *Well begun is half done,* as the saying goes, and you will find it worth your time to undertake at least some of the following activities.

- Visit your campus student employment center to learn more about internships. Although fieldwork is not exactly the same as an internship with a company, there are similarities. Find out what responsibilities internships involve. How many hours does the typical internship require of students? What skills are prerequisites? What can students expect to learn from these? (Pay special attention to internships offered for "credit"— as these are often likely to stress what students can expect to get out of the internship.)

- Get to know your campus library better (or public library, if there is one nearby), as well as you know your own home. You will waste an awful lot of (very limited) time and effort searching for things if you do not know where to look for them. Navigate the library to learn where to find general business publications. Where are references located? Periodicals (current and not-so-recent)? Computer databases (learn what you can search for on these, and whether any on-line charges for using Internet or other databases are imposed). Find out if there is a librarian or other staff member who specializes in small business areas (and learn his or her name and phone extension).

• Obtain copies of previous fieldwork projects, or samples of these, to familiarize yourself with what an end product should resemble. Most professors will only show you those cases of which they are most proud. You will be able to hold a quality piece of work and discover what made it so.

• Talk to other students who have engaged in fieldwork. If you don't know of any, ask a professor who administers fieldwork to put you in contact with one. Better yet, talk to several students. This will give you a broader, more realistic perspective because you won't be limited to the advice and reactions of a student who might have had an extreme experience that was great or terrible.

• Visit your local Small Business Administration, Small Business Development Center, or any other entrepreneurial or small business public or private sector agency. Find out what materials they may have for you to read or hear. If your city or town does not have such an agency, write to the SBA (see Chapter 5 for more information on contacting other organizations).

• Visit your local Chamber of Commerce. Chambers are excellent repositories of information on the local business community, and are representative of the concerns and issues that face business owners in the area. You might even attend a meeting or other event sponsored by the Chamber. Incidentally, this can yield a big payoff later in the contacts you will have established through networking with members of a Chamber.

READY . . . SET . . .

Congratulations on choosing to participate in fieldwork. Get ready for an educational experience that is second to none. It will require your energy, commitment, and flexibility. Through it all, your confidence will increase as you sharpen your business skills on some real-world problems. Don't expect to have all the answers. You may, in fact, refer your client to some seasoned experts in a particular area (a computer software designer, for example) for help that you can't provide. The mark of an effective consultant is being open and complete with what you do know, and admitting what you do not. This is the most any fieldwork client can ask of you.

Good luck! The next chapter deals with what fieldwork is and what it isn't, as you embark on your consulting project with an entrepreneur of a real business.

REFERENCES

Buller, P. F. (1992). Reconceptualizing the small business consulting course: A response to the Porter and McKibbin criticisms. *Journal of Management Education, 16*(1), 56-75.

Fry, F. L. (1985). The determinants of successful SBI projects from the academic perspective. *Proceedings of the Small Business Institute Directors' Association,* 32-37.

Kiesner, W. F. (1987). A study of SBI client satisfaction levels. *Proceedings of the Small Business Institute Directors' Association,* 271-276.

Kolb, D., Lublin, S., Spoth, J., & Baker, R. (1987). Strategic management development: Using experiential learning theory to assess and develop managerial competencies. *Journal of Management Development, 5,* 13-24.

O'Connor, E. L., & Rogers, J. C. (1988). An examination of the attitudes of clients and students in the SBI case situation. *Proceedings of the Small Business Institute Directors' Association,* 311-315.

Ramocki, S. (1987). Measured effectiveness of client-sponsored projects in the marketing research course. *Journal of Marketing Education, 9,* 24-30.

Robichaux, M. (1990, February 22). Small firms are taking lessons from college kids. *Wall Street Journal,* pp. B1-B2.

Weinstein, A., Nicholls, J.A.F., & Seaton, B. (1992, October). An evaluation of SBI marketing consulting: The entrepreneur's perspective. *Journal of Small Business Management,* pp. 62-71.

2 | The Fieldwork Experience
What It Is and What It Isn't

Quick Tips

- Make sure you begin your field consulting case with realistic expectations about what can happen.
- Certain cases just don't lead to good fieldwork experiences. Among these are cases that are primarily clerical tasks or ones that require a highly sophisticated set of skills not normally provided by student consultants.
- Typical fieldwork projects include conducting a feasibility analysis for a proposed business, developing a business plan for an existing business, searching for a new location, conducting market research for a new or modified product or service, creating advertising strategies to increase market share, identifying sources of funding for growth or expansion, and updating a financial plan.
- Review the 10 myths about field case consulting. They will help you realize, for example, that a business with no obvious problems can be an exceptional opportunity for a good case experience, the "best" clients are not necessarily entrepreneurial types in the classic sense, and working in a group can be an important learning experience.

Fieldwork, like any work, means different things to different people. This chapter presents examples of what appropriate fieldwork is and some persistent common myths about fieldwork. The purpose is to help you develop *realistic* expectations about fieldwork so that you can proceed through the consulting experience with fewer surprises.

WHAT IS APPROPRIATE FIELDWORK?

Fieldwork can be a component of many courses, departments, and curricula. It can be a relatively minor part of a course that includes other written work and examinations—or, it can be the only component of a course, the one on which your entire grade is based. The type of fieldwork you do is dependent on which of the above sets of criteria it fulfills. So what makes a project appropriate? Let's start with what probably does not make a good fieldwork experience:

A project that is primarily clerical in nature; that is, you are asked to file, to do data entry, to answer telephones and other activities that have little to do with a substantive business problem (for both client and students), and everything to do with the client desperately needing administrative help.

The other extreme: a project that is far too complex, or relies on highly sophisticated, specialized knowledge that is beyond the norm of what student consultants can provide. Knowing what you *can't* do for your client is just as valuable as knowing what you can do. If your client tells you she or he needs advice or activities performed that are beyond your ken, *speak up early!* It will cause you far less embarrassment to admit your limits at the start of the project than it will to bluff your way through and produce an unacceptable end product.

Another example is a project in which the entrepreneur is not open to the suggestions or comments of the students from the get-go. This not only hinders the creative process in assisting the business with its problems, but creates a negative educational experience for the students involved in the case.

Consider the "dribble" type of project as a problem. The client may be disorganized or detail-oriented to the extent that the project goals dribble out a little at a time as you get involved. These are sometimes called "moving target" cases: The project goals change drastically from what they were at the onset. Be aware, however, that a change may mean that the client becomes cognizant of what is really important to the business as the case matures, and it is your work in progress that in fact enables the client to see more clearly and accurately what needs to be done. This example would be an appropriate learning experience as you sharpen your problem identification skills. What we mean by inappropriate is, for example, the project that jumps around (Tuesday it's this goal, Wednesday it's that one) with no rationale or evidence for change. And, chances are good that the client will not be satisfied with anything you do, because he or she hasn't the slightest idea of what to work on anyway. This latter example we urge you to treat like a bed of hot coals— don't touch it and seek help from your instructor or project adviser.

Fieldwork is appropriate when it *directly relates* to what you are doing in the course or in related courses in your program. If you are asked to complete a market analysis or construct a business plan, chances are very good that these tasks are immediate to what you are doing in your coursework in business school. Being asked to design a new software program, however, may not be. If you are unclear about the connection between the Project Purpose and your course objectives, ask your professor or the case coordinator early on. It shouldn't require a stretch on anyone's part to see the connection between the fieldwork and coursework.

Appropriate fieldwork should bring you into close contact with businesses. Although projects that rely exclusively on research conducted at the library may have their value to some clients, as professors we could do this just as well by assigning a term paper as a project, and wouldn't call this fieldwork. Using the library is an integral part of fieldwork, but it must not be the only activity. Getting out into the "trenches," into real businesses and meeting real founders, managers, and employees, is the heart of the matter of fieldwork. Even if you see much of your fieldwork time being time spent collecting information in the library, try to find some way to collect information through interviews in real businesses as well.

Up to now we have talked mostly about fieldwork that is part of formal coursework. It should be noted that more students are now taking the initiative to set up their own, outside-of-course fieldwork projects. Many see this as an opportunity to get practical experience for themselves, for the reasons discussed in Chapter 1. Others are driven by an interest in a particular business or industry that they wish to learn more about through immersion. Certainly these projects constitute appropriate fieldwork. Students who elect to engage in fieldwork on their own would be well advised to seek guidance from individual faculty or staff members at the university as they carry out their projects.

SOME TYPICAL FIELDWORK PROJECTS

Field cases encompass a broad range of activities. Here is just a sampling of the kinds of tasks that students have been asked to undertake:

• Perform a feasibility analysis for a proposed business. This involves analyzing the external environment, a market analysis, interviews with prospective customers, an industry analysis, and projections of financial requirements and performance.

• Develop a business plan for an existing business. This includes at least the following areas: Description of the product(s) or service(s) and market(s); operations; organization and management approaches; and financial requirements, performance, and projections.

• Conduct a location analysis for a business that is considering a geographic move. This may mean conducting a transportation/traffic analysis, investigating leasing arrangements, checking out available commercial space, and so on.

• Test the market for a new product or service. Establish prospective consumer groups, conduct focus group sessions, give samples and record reactions; determine what the market is willing to pay, and what potential or actual customers demand be improved.

• Develop advertising strategies to increase market share or awareness. This usually involves creative tasks such as coming up with alternative methods to capture customer interest and observing what competitors' strategies are.

- Identify potential sources of funding for growth or expansion. Locate and evaluate the many sources of capital that entrepreneurs and managers can access; help get the firm's financial house in order.

SOME COMMON MYTHS ABOUT FIELDWORK

Myth 1. A business with no obvious problems makes for a poor field case.

Most students are accustomed to analyzing written (textbook) cases that have noticeable, specific problems and issues to be addressed. Some come with a set of questions attached to them, cuing students about what to focus on for case analysis. Because most of you have spent considerable time analyzing such cases, it is not unusual to expect your fieldwork case to be similar—that is, to have visible, obvious problems that need to be solved. Some cases do, but a "good" case need not be rife with impending disaster, insolvency, poor leadership, or lousy products and services. In fact, "good" cases are likely to involve firms that are in healthy financial (and other) shape. It's just that the founder/owner/manager thinks that it could be even better. What's more, just because the problems are not obvious, they can still exist. Learning how to become an effective fieldwork "sleuth" is just one of the many skills you are on your way to enhancing.

Myth 2. Students can save a business from failure.

If you do work on a case that exhibits serious problems, it is often irresistible to want to believe that you can, in classic guardian angel fashion, come to the rescue of the business and save it from imminent (or even not so imminent) failure. Unfortunately, this myth is often held by clients, who think that a last-ditch attempt to fix what went wrong by contracting with students will avoid the inevitable for them and their businesses. Be on the alert for symptoms of the "guardian angel syndrome" in clients. If you pick up cues that their expectations are unrealistic, address this early in the case. Ask them what it is they expect you to do or to find out, and what impact that is likely to have on the business. Let them know that, as much as you appreciate their faith in your abilities, you cannot fix in several weeks what took months or years to get that way. Inform your instructor of the situation.

Myth 3. The "best" clients are wild-eyed entrepreneurial or managerial types.

You will find that clients' management styles vary tremendously. In most entrepreneurship and small business courses, some time is spent discussing characteristics, traits, and behaviors associated with business owners and key managers. It is natural, then, that students entering fieldwork in small businesses want to experience the thrill of working with and for a wild-eyed inventor or classic entrepreneur. Truth is, both wild-eyed clients and the buttoned-down variety are "good" clients—they just go about it differently. The *innovators* may be very interested in brainstorming with students about ideas; they probably will give them the project in a very unstructured manner, urging the students to go off and find their own way of doing the project tasks. Such individuals can be exciting to be around: Their enthusiasm and passion for their product/service is infectious, and meetings are spirited and lively, with many ideas and solutions pouring into the conversation at once. No doubt you will learn much from such individuals, such as creative approaches to problem solving and how to make work "fun." But the client who is less adventurous and is reticent about sharing off-the-wall ideas does have other things to offer you. Such individuals are likely to be very good at evaluating and implementing solutions. They are also more likely to structure the project (so that it's manageable), to seek and give feedback, and seek out and give interim evaluations. In short, they are not likely to leave you hanging, and you will usually know exactly what to do, when, and how to do it. Though they may not prefer to make sweeping changes in their businesses, they do know how to make things work. As stabilizers, they can help you learn how to take an idea (that a "wild-eyed" type may have conceived) and refine and reproduce it.

Myth 4. "Good" fieldwork cases are broad, with many objectives.

Sometimes students worry that unless a case has many goals and activities to carry out, there will be a shortage of things to do, and the resulting report will not contain anything of major impact or interest. Actually, it is probably difficult to make a project narrow enough, so that students can be assured of their ability to complete it within the allotted time frame. Remember, if you can focus your problem appropriately, you can do a much more effective in-depth analysis of it that is more likely to have an effect on the business. Tackling too many issues at once, even if they are delegated within the group, can lead to a cursory analysis with the critical problem given short shrift as a result. In the worst scenario, a superficial, inadequate analysis of many issues could lead the entrepreneur mistakenly to implement the wrong solution. Our advice: *do more work on fewer problems* in fieldwork.

Myth 5. It's better (more expedient) to work alone than in a group in fieldwork.

In classes or in work settings, most of us have had negative experiences with groups. In some instances this was because we felt that others in the group did not do their fair share of the work, because members didn't get along, or because the group was not motivated to reach its goal. These feelings can lead to great frustration and performance that falls far short of expectations. So why not be resolved to complete your fieldwork on your own, rather than with other students in class? Now consider this correlation: *The more important the issue or project, the more likely a group is needed to solve or work on it!*

Groups are very effective at raising different perspectives on a problem or issue. The more heterogenous groups are, that is, the more the members have different than alike backgrounds, the better they are at raising these perspectives. The sheer number of ideas that are generated by groups, compared with individuals, is much larger. The more people there are in a group, the more person-hours there are available to solve problems and tackle a wider range of issues because group members' skills will complement one another. Most of us will be working in groups throughout our lives, so it makes good career sense to learn how to be a more effective group member and leader. *Group Smarts* are survival skills— plain and simple. Watch for your pre-group expectations, however. You tend to get what you expect (and what you put in). So if you have decided a priori that your fieldwork group is likely to be as ineffective and frustrating as the last group you worked in, chances are very good that—surprise—it will be! This is because you will invest very little of your own effort and interest in the group (which other members can pick up quicker than a hound can a scented trail), and the result will be a lousy group experience and a low-quality project. If you are concerned about all members receiving one group grade regardless of input quality, suggest to your fieldwork professor that a team member evaluation form be a weighted component of your course grade, if it is not already. Peer

evaluations on degree of participation, preparation, quality, and interpersonal skills that are counted toward each member's course grade will
go a long way toward raising the motivation of all students to work hard
on behalf of the group.

Here's what some students had to say about their (mis)conceptions
about working in groups:

> "Seeing different people in a similar situation tackling similar
> problems in different ways is very enlightening, proving there is no
> one correct way to operate a business."

> "When I first got the chance to meet my partners, they seemed like
> pretty good people to get along with, but there was the old 'group
> conflict' thing in my head. I was asking myself, 'Who would be the
> leader?' 'Who would be the followers?' and 'Who would give every-
> one else problems?' Surprisingly, no one person was the leader, but
> we were all leaders in our own way! I felt that this was a good sign
> considering that we were all strangers."

> "Everyone in our group accepted the role of an involved par-
> ticipant, rather than that of a disinterested observer who has no
> stake or interest in resolving the problems in question. Because of
> my group's enthusiasm, I personally was even more compelled to
> contribute a lot. I became extremely dedicated to my teammates
> and to the overall success of our project."

One student offered this guidance to working effectively in groups:

> "In cases, the members who are contributing more should always
> make an extra effort to get the other members involved because it
> is not fair to be so motivated that you smother the ideas and
> contributions of someone who is just plain shy. In real-life situa-
> tions, members need to complement each other and make up for
> any weaknesses that exist in the other members."

*Myth 6. It's better (more fun, more efficient) to form my own group with
friends than with other students whom I don't yet know.*

If you admit that you believed in Myth 5, then you may be inclined to soften your anticipated gloom-and-doom of group work by electing to work with a team of friends in class. Why not, you might think? After all, you already know these individuals: their styles, preferences, habits. The reason that working with a hand-picked group of friends may not lead to the best fieldwork experience is that you will find it much harder to rock the boat and confront differences with them on project issues than you would with a group of others whom you don't know so well. We have known groups consisting of friends that have ended in conflict and with friendships terminated, with much bad feeling spread around. But, more relevant to the workplace: Individuals in organizations are not assigned to task groups on the basis of friendship, but instead based on the type of contribution they can best make to meet the needs of the group.

In addition, you have more to learn from people whom you don't know, whose ideas and perceptions may be different and unfamiliar to you. Are you still resisting the idea of joining a team of "strangers?" Aha! You've just made a pre-group assumption before you have even met them. Reread Myth 5.

Myth 7. A business that is more established makes a better fieldwork case than a start-up or pre-start-up business.

An already established business does have at least some records, archives, and policies to read, observe, and use as a starting point for the project. Many fieldwork cases are such businesses, considering perhaps a change in strategy, product, or market. But don't judge these as more interesting or even more appropriate to a fieldwork assignment. The business that is still an idea in someone's head, or that has just recently opened its doors, also makes an excellent field study. The younger the business, the less likely that established precedents exist, along with all the constraints in creative thinking (e.g., the "We've never done it this way before, so why would it work now?" mentality) that accompany such practices. Consider any case an opportunity for you. New-business cases allow you to set direction for the ownership, to try many alternative proposals for decisions, and (what many students find most enjoyable) to be able to visit the business a few months later, after its opening, to see some of your recommendations in action.

Myth 8. The more exciting the business (or product or service) seems, the more interesting the fieldwork will be.

Some cases come with descriptions of business products or services that sound glamorous and exciting, in industries that are "hot" or associated with entrepreneurs who are "hot." Some will indeed be so. But don't apply this generalization too liberally. For example, not too long ago a student team was given a case involving an inventor who was designing a new video-based sports-training system. The students were promised that they could make several visits to a local sports team stadium, meet several key players on the team who were going to test this new system, and test the marketability of the product. Not surprisingly, their classmates thought that this case was much more interesting than any other in the class that term, and became envious . . . for a while. It soon played out that the inventor was in the midst of several projects and couldn't be bothered to meet with the students more than once during the entire term. What's more, the students never did get invited to the sports stadium at all, and were left doing library research with no cause to ever leave campus to finish their case. As it turned out, the only envy in that class was felt by the students assigned to the sports entrepreneur who were left with a mundane case with little learning to offer them. Be assured, however, that very few clients ever have the temerity to be no-shows to their students and to renege on the relationship in this way.

Myth 9. All of the ideas I recommend to the client should be put into practice.

Agreed, there is frustration in taking the time to come up with some very useful ideas and action steps, only to have them rejected, or worse, ignored by the business owner or manager. All consultants take this risk. But remember your job description: Your role as a student consultant is to analyze a problem or set of issues and generate recommendations to be put to the client for consideration. You are not judged on, or responsible for, whether the client actually puts these into practice in the business. There may be factors about which you are unaware that would make an idea infeasible (e.g., cost, skills and talents of the entrepreneur, time, and so on) for business practice. Even if the idea is a great one, the entrepreneur may have personal reasons (mistrust, fear, procrastination, finding another idea more appealing, etc.) for lack of action. This is OK.

You will be evaluated on fieldwork process, and you have no control over which ideas are put in place in the field organization. But take heart: It is very likely that at least some of your ideas will work their way into the business. (Increase the odds that they will, by reading Chapter 6 very carefully.) Consider this student's experience:

> "There were ideas that were informally mentioned to the client during periodic meetings, which the client did not seem responsive toward, and there were some ideas that she readily accepted and put into action before the team had produced the Final Report. One instance of this was when she was told about ways in which she could improve her sidewalk sign, and she immediately took action —which created a positive feeling for the group."

Myth 10. I can fit fieldwork assignments into my schedule after I fulfill my obligations to other courses, jobs, exercise, or other activities in my life.
Most of us have many roles and obligations to fulfill. But be fore-warned that to think of fieldwork as an activity that can be squeezed in, postponed, or otherwise subordinate to your schedule is a mistaken conception. If you prefer classes where no outside work is expected, then fieldwork is not for you. Your fieldwork professor realizes that you have other commitments in your life besides the consulting case, but it is up to you to exercise excellent time management skills. Accept the challenge, as this student demonstrated:

> "The aspect of the live case that was so educational was the freedom from applied structure. In the real world, people are not there to take care of you. A person must make her own schedule to meet deadlines. The live cases offered the chance for teams to motivate themselves, set their own time limits."

View the calendar not as an enemy, but as an opportunity to set direction for yourself in the project. Design an outline or schedule during the first week of fieldwork so you and your group know exactly what should be completed by what deadline. Periodically review this schedule to see if you are meeting your targets. Do not relegate your assignments to the last few days or weeks of the term. You will avoid a lot of stress, angry fellow team members, and a shoddy project report by applying some time management sense to the fieldwork. Set a schedule, ask for assistance when necessary, and, above all, be a proactive consultant.

3 | Managing the Fieldwork

Quick Tips

- Develop good project management techniques—and use them!
- Collect any information your professor or project coordinator has obtained prior to the start of your fieldwork.
- Use the PEST framework (shown in Figure 3.2) to analyze the firm's general environment, and visit the client to get a "feel" for the firm.
- Establish a professional image—first impressions last long.
- In early meetings with the client, establish what to do (Project Purpose); how to do it (action plan); and what to provide the client (results).
- Include an Executive Summary in your report—the client will read this word for word.
- For the final client presentation, prepare visual aids in bulleted form, and practice, practice, practice.
- Allow for ongoing communication and follow-up with the client.

The key to the success of the fieldwork experience—for both the students and the client organization—is in the management of the fieldwork. It is impossible to emphasize this point enough: *Good project management techniques are essential.* Too many students believe they can "muddle through" and somehow, when the deadline nears, pull together a stellar project. In our experience, nothing could be further from the

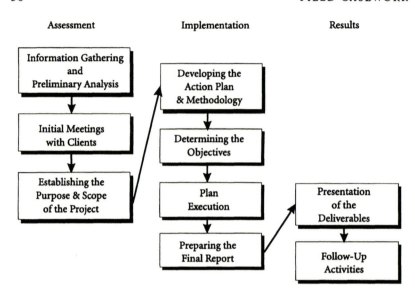

Figure 3.1. Managing the Fieldwork: A Process Model

truth. Success comes from planning the fieldwork process, organizing the members of the consulting team, directing the activities of the team, and controlling the efforts of team members throughout the project.

To assist in managing the fieldwork project, it is useful to consider the process model shown in Figure 3.1. This model presents the key elements in the fieldwork project in a "flowchart process" format. We will use this model as the basis for developing an understanding of the issues involved in managing the fieldwork process, and will constantly refer to the model throughout this chapter.

THE ASSESSMENT PHASE

The initial stage of the fieldwork process is the assessment phase. During the assessment phase, the student consulting team will gather information about the client firm, the general and industry environment of the client firm, and the nature of the project itself. The team will meet with the client and will try to identify the client's needs and the scope of the proposed project. The outcome is a determination of the project

Deliverables—the results that the team will be expected to present to the client.

Fieldwork projects do not generally come in a "ready-to-be-written" format. By nature, projects are often vague and ambiguous. It is not uncommon for the initial client request to be as general as "developing a business plan," "help with marketing," or "assistance in running my business better." Therefore, the first problem the team confronts is to determine what must be done to assist the client.

INFORMATION GATHERING
AND PRELIMINARY ANALYSES

The first step in the fieldwork process is Information Gathering and Preliminary Analyses. Even before the student consulting team has an opportunity to meet with the client, it is beneficial for the team members to do some up-front work gathering information about the client and the proposed project. A little preliminary preparation pays substantial dividends in "getting up to speed" on the project.

To facilitate the information-gathering process, the instructor or project coordinator should meet with the client firm prior to accepting the project. At this meeting, the client should identify the nature of the proposed project and provide a brief description of the client and the industry. Any information the client has obtained—franchise information, prospectus, market research, brochures, and so on—should be copied and furnished to the student consulting team.

These data will serve as the basis for the student consulting team's initial information-gathering activities. Based on the client's indicated request for consultation, the student team should gather information on three important elements: the General Environment, the Industry Environment, and the Client Firm.

The General Environment. The general environment is the larger context in which the client firm operates or seeks to conduct business. There are many models that have been developed to assess the general environment (Pearce & Robinson, 1994; Thompson & Strickland, 1995). Any of these frameworks can be used by the consulting team. The important point is that the team have a framework in mind and utilize the framework in conducting the information search.

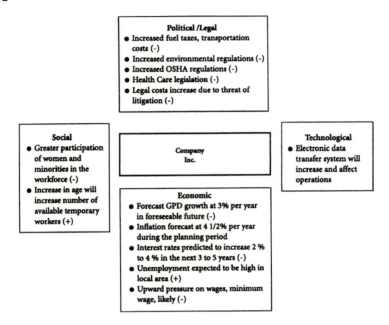

Figure 3.2. PEST Model

One framework that we prefer is the PEST framework (see Figure 3.2). The general environment is seen as having four dimensions: Political/Legal issues, Economic issues, Social/Demographic issues, and Technological issues. Each of these can be expected to have some influence on the client firm. The student team should gather information about each of these four dimensions as a basis for developing an understanding of the broad context in which the client firm operates.

Political/legal issues include federal, state, and local laws and regulations that affect the client firm or the industry. Among the more notable topics that should be considered are tax laws and regulations, environmental policies, local ordinances, employment laws, and government policies toward small business. Also, teams should consider the effects of political trends on the client firm's operations, such as changes in the regulatory environment or pending legislation that may affect the client's business. Patent and copyright laws may be another area of analysis. Trade laws—particularly import/export regulations, tariffs, trade barriers, and the like—affect more and more firms in the global marketplace and may need to be considered. At the local level, such issues as health laws, zoning regulations, and business permits should be examined. The amount of government regulation that affects businesses is substantial, and consulting teams need to perform extensive research to evaluate and appreciate fully the magnitude of the political, legal, and regulatory issues.

Economic issues are concerned with the effects of changes in the macro-economic forces that can be expected to affect the client firm. These might include growth in Gross Domestic Product (GDP), business cycles, unemployment data, purchasing indices, and other key economic indicators. It is important to note that these issues need to be analyzed at a level relevant to the client firm's proposed project. It doesn't make sense to gather information on national unemployment levels if the client intends to do business in a specific area or region. Information must be applicable to the client's activities.

Social/demographic forces are those trends in a society that could be expected to influence the client's operations. Population trends in aging, income levels, purchasing habits, consumer attitudes, and similar demographic and psychographic data can be useful in understanding the dynamics that underlie the client's markets or business. As with economic data, this information should be gathered for the relevant area of the client firm's operations.

Technology refers to the body of knowledge about a particular subject. It is more than just new hardware and physical equipment. Technology can include any new information or knowledge that affects the way people behave. The consulting team needs to examine the nature of the client's request and ask, "What new facts, data, or knowledge have been or will be developed that will have an effect on this firm's activities?" In addition, the team should also consider the rate of technological change. Some businesses are fairly stable: The way these firms conduct their operations does not change much from year to year, such as movie theaters. Other firms confront situations of rapid technological change, such as computer software companies. In cases of high technological turbulence, analyzing the effects of technology on the client firm will be difficult.

The Industry Environment. An industry is a group of firms that produce products or services that are similar in nature and are intended to satisfy a common, defined demand. The industry environment is thought of as being contained within the larger general environmental context and consists of those forces that can be expected to influence the specific product-market of the client firm. Determining the industry boundaries is one of the first decisions that must be made in performing the analysis.

Once the industry is defined, the team can use various alternative models to examine systematically the effects of industry forces on the client firm. One such model is the use of concentration ratios to determine if the industry is highly concentrated (oligopolistic) or fragmented in nature. Patterns of competition tend to vary depending on the concentration of the industry. Another popular method is to examine the stage of the industry life cycle to determine if the industry is in the introduction, growth, maturity, or decline stage.

Perhaps the most popular method is Michael Porter's (1980) model (see Figure 3.3). Porter identifies five forces that affect competition within industries: Threat of Substitute Products, Threat of New Entry, Bargaining Power of Suppliers, Bargaining Power of Buyers, and Competitive Rivalry. Each of these five forces is influenced by a number of underlying structural determinants. The relative strength of these five forces affects the competitiveness of the industry and the profitability of firms within an industry.

As with the general environment, the essential point is that the student team gather information about the client firm's industry and organize the information in a systematic manner that will allow the team to understand the nature of the client's business. It is axiomatic that good consultation requires that the consultant has a reasonably good comprehension of the conditions and forces that affect the client organization. Without a knowledge of the client firm's environment, the consultant is likely to draw conclusions and make recommendations that are not practical or useful.

The Client Firm. The final element that needs analysis is the client firm. Sometimes, the field project calls for examination of a new business opportunity: The client may be an entrepreneur who as yet has not established an organization. In such cases, this analysis can be omitted. If, however, the client firm is one that is currently in operation, the consulting team should make an effort to gather some preliminary information on the organization.

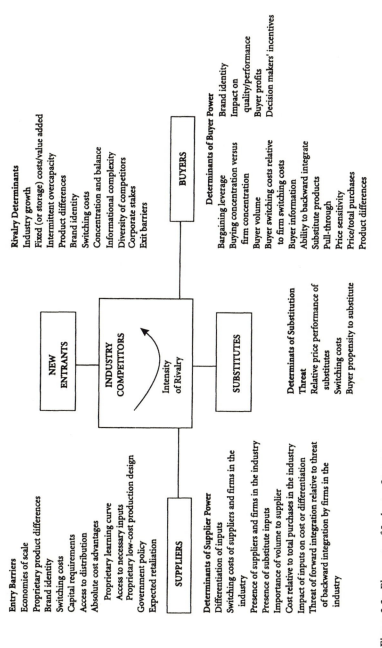

Figure 3.3. Elements of Industry Structure

SOURCE: Reprinted with the permission of The Free Press, an imprint of Simon & Schuster from *Competitive Strategy: Techniques for Analyzing Industries and Competitors* by Michael E. Porter. Copyright © 1980 by the Free Press..

At this stage of the fieldwork process, it is not reasonable to expect that the team will gather comprehensive data. Instead, the team should concentrate on getting a general "feel" for the client firm. A visit to the client firm as a potential customer—where feasible—can provide insights about the firm's daily operations. Discussions with customers or competitors can also provide insights on perceptions of the client firm and are a useful source of information. The main point is that the consulting team should have an awareness of the client firm's scope of activity and basic methods of business prior to meeting the client.

Preliminary Analysis. It is important to emphasize again that the information-gathering process is to be done prior to the Initial Meeting With the Client. Thus, it is often useful to specify that the consulting team attempt to gather as much information as possible without having direct contact with the client. In our experience, this is useful for two reasons: First, it allows the consulting team to concentrate on a comprehensive analysis of secondary information without possible bias injected by the client; and second, it prepares the student team for the initial client meeting.

The actual methods the team can use to gather the data are described in more detail in Chapter 5. For our purposes in explaining the fieldwork process here, the key issue is for the team to gather the information and then to perform a preliminary analysis of the client organization. What are the major forces that operate in support of the client firm or project, and what forces are in opposition? What is the overall impression of the client firm? Is the industry highly profitable or highly competitive? Is the industry growing or is it mature? These and many other questions should be discussed by the members of the team prior to the Initial Meeting With the Client. Where possible, a preliminary analysis can be prepared for presentation to the client at the Initial Meeting.

The importance of gathering information and conducting the preliminary analysis cannot be overemphasized. For most students, the fieldwork project is the first experience with organization consultation. There is bound to be a certain amount of fear and nervousness as the student realizes that the advice that will be given to the client is not a classroom exercise or case analysis, but is going to be taken seriously by the client and will be used by the client to make actual business decisions. One client once told one of our teams at the initial counseling session,

"You are going to help me determine what I'm going to do with the next five years of my life—do I invest in a new business opportunity or stay in my present job?" Faced with such a task, student consultants can easily become afraid of giving bad information, which often leads to a safe— but less than optimal—recommendation.

Because the Objective of the fieldwork counseling is to give the best possible business advice, it is essential that the student consulting team try to optimize the process. One of the best ways to begin this is through up-front Information Gathering and the Preliminary Analyses. Having a working knowledge of the client or the industry improves the consultants' self-confidence and provides a basis for intelligent discussions with the client—the next step in the assessment phase.

INITIAL MEETINGS WITH THE CLIENT

Once the student consulting team has gathered information from secondary sources about the client firm and the environment and has conducted a preliminary analysis, it is time to meet the client face to face and begin the fieldwork consultation process. This is an exciting time for both the client and the consulting team. The consulting team is looking forward to actually meeting the client and learning firsthand about the client's needs and concerns. The client is anxious to have the team begin work to address the client's needs and concerns. Both are usually uncertain as to what to expect from each other; in most instances, each is experiencing the process for the first time.

Recognize that both the consulting team and the client are often faced with time pressures. Students are generally taking other classes in addition to the fieldwork project; some may be in the process of finishing their education experience and are preparing for graduation and new jobs, interviews, and so on. The typical client is also very busy—most managers, particularly those in small businesses, are trying to perform multiple roles in running the company, managing their personal life, attending meetings, and carrying out a host of other regular activities. Thus, it is important to make sure that the time spent in actual face-to-face meetings is productive.

The Initial Meeting. The Initial Meeting should be held at a neutral site, such as the sponsoring college or university or perhaps the local small business development center, if one is available. This enables the team and the client to begin the relationship in a professional manner, free from distractions that may be inherent in the client's business operations. For example, it is hard to have an effective meeting at the client's place of business if the phone is ringing or customers and employees are interrupting. At a neutral site, the client and the consulting team are free to concentrate on the project and can get the process off to a good start.

Project coordinators should meet in advance with the client and provide a realistic preview of the fieldwork project. Included in this preview are a description of the fieldwork project and process, expectations regarding the client's support of the team, information on the expected time frame and project management, and procedural matters pertaining to project administration. This will help prepare the client for the Initial Meeting with the students.

The members of the consulting team should be encouraged to appear at the Initial Meeting in a professional manner. Suits or coats and ties for men and professional apparel for women are good standards. The team has only one chance to create a first impression on the client; the impression should be a positive one. If students show up for the meeting dressed in T-shirts, sweatshirts, and blue jeans (in other words, typical student dress), the initial impression formed by the client is that the team is a bunch of "college kids." This is an image that the team will have to work to overcome for the rest of the project, and it can hamper the team's effectiveness in working with the client. If, on the other hand, the team sets a professional tone at the outset, it will be much easier to maintain a positive working relationship during the course of the project. Often, a client will tell students that such apparel is not necessary in the future, in which case the team should honor the client's request. But the first impression will still have been made!

The project coordinator or faculty advisor may want to attend the meeting, but we would advise against this practice. In our experience, clients tend to talk to the faculty member rather than the student team, detracting attention from the purpose of the meeting. Alternatively, the team members may feel somewhat restricted or intimidated by having a faculty member present, especially when their grade is at stake. To have the best possible interaction, the meeting should be between the client and the consultants only. The consultants can summarize the results of the meeting for the faculty advisor at a later date.

The team leader should introduce the team members, and everyone should become acquainted with one another. If the team has prepared written assessments of the environment and industry, these should be presented to the client early in the meeting. The client will generally be impressed that the team has already done some preliminary work and will tend to view the team more favorably. One useful technique to get the conversation under way is for the team to ask the client questions based on the preliminary analyses. If there are any issues about which team members are uncertain, they can ask the client for information and for answers to specific questions. This not only allows the team to obtain additional information, it allows the client to become involved early in the project.

The client should then be given an opportunity to describe to the team the expectations and issues the client has regarding the project. Clients should be encouraged to bring in information or samples of the type of work or service that the firm provides. A brief background or history of the project is also useful. Once these "exploratory" and "prefatory" issues are out of the way, the discussion can move on to more substantive matters.

Perhaps the most significant issue that should be discussed at the Initial Meeting is the client's expectations for the project. What does the client want to have done by the team? What are the types of issues for which assistance is sought? What are the questions that the client would like to have answered by the team? How does the client envision the nature and scope of the project? These are very important issues and will frame the balance of the fieldwork project. The members of the consulting team need to be attentive to the client's needs and expectations.

Once these issues are out on the table, the major purpose of the Initial Meeting has been met. At this point, it is appropriate for the team to try to schedule a second meeting with the client to discuss the client's needs, the Purpose of the Project, and the scope of the team's activities. If the client's place of business is available, the second meeting should take place there. This allows the students a chance to get additional firsthand insights on the client's operations and needs. For many projects, this is not possible; the project may be a new venture or may be one that the client wishes to keep separate from other business activities or relationships. In such cases, a mutually agreeable site and time should be arranged by the team and the client.

The Second Meeting. There are two major Objectives for the second meeting with the client. The first is to allow the student consulting team to observe the client's place of business and operations in order to develop a "feel" for the type of activities that occur within the client's firm. This firsthand experience is important, because it gives the consulting team a sense of the client's company that is not possible from secondhand information. The visit also tends to improve communication between the team and the client, because the site visit experience provides a common frame of reference: Both parties now have a shared knowledge of the client's business, which forms a basis for future discussions. Effective consulting requires that the consultant develop a thorough understanding of the client, and there is little substitute for an actual "on-site" visit to facilitate this process.

The second Objective of the meeting is for the student consulting team to focus on the client's specific needs as a basis for determining the Purpose and Scope of the Project. At the Initial Meeting, both parties are usually occupied with introductions and exchanging information with one another. Even though the client may have a general idea of the type of project desired, the actual determination of the Project Purpose must be made through a process of discussion and negotiation. The second meeting is an ideal time to begin this activity.

ESTABLISHING THE PURPOSE
AND SCOPE OF THE PROJECT

Determining the Client's Needs. One of the most important activities performed by the student team occurs very early in the project: establishing the Purpose of the Project. The Purpose guides the student team during the remainder of the consulting project and determines the amount of effort and the quality of the final project. It pays to take time at the start of the project to determine and specify the Project Purpose carefully.

The student team has had a chance to review the information obtained from the Initial Meeting and may have a preliminary concept of the nature of the project. It is necessary to refine this into a clear statement of purpose that is satisfactory to both the client and the student team. To do so, it is first necessary to identify the client's needs.

One problem that consulting teams frequently encounter is that the client may not have a good idea of his or her needs. The client's request for assistance often may be vague and general, such as "I need help developing a business plan," "I need to know more about my customers," or "I need to know how to improve my business." Although these may be accurate perceptions from the client's perspective, such statements do not give the consultants much direction! Almost any type of assistance could be offered in such circumstances.

Therefore, one of the first things the consulting team should try to do is to determine the client's specific needs. In what areas of operations does the client seem to be deficient or to require assistance? Given the nature of the client's business, what are the key items of information that are needed about the market, customers, or competitors to allow the client to make good business decisions? What are the necessary elements of a good business plan, and what needs to be done to acquire these elements? The more specific the identification of the client's needs, the better will be the Project Purpose. The team should ask, "What information does the client need?" "What is the outcome the client wants—advice, assistance, information, support?" "What are the major problems that the client needs to have resolved?" "What are the decisions that the client needs to make?" These and similar questions will help the team to identify properly the client's needs.

Student teams often find that the client may have many needs; so many, in fact, that the team cannot possibly address each one in the time frame allotted for the project. In such cases, the team needs to exercise good judgment and prioritize the client's needs. Are there some areas of concern that will have a significant impact on the client's operations? Is there a sequential nature to the various needs—that is, do some issues logically come ahead of others? (For example, it may be necessary to perform a market analysis prior to developing a business plan.) Issues that are high impact or that logically precede other needs should be given a high priority by the consulting team.

In addition, the team needs to compare the client's needs with the resources available to the team—both in time and in individual skills. It is important for the team to be committed to providing the client with the best possible quality of advice and information. If the team does not have sufficient time or lacks the skills necessary to address the client's need(s) effectively, this should be communicated to the client. It is better to limit the scope of the project and produce a high-quality result than to promise too much and offer poor advice. Thus, the client's needs should be matched with the team's abilities to determine the Purpose of the Project.

Although the team may perform a preliminary needs assessment, the actual determination of the Project Purpose and Scope results from a process of negotiation between the two parties. The team should suggest to the client a tentative Purpose that describes the needs to be addressed by the team, the resources the team is prepared to commit to the project, and the information or advice the team intends to provide to the client. These should be reviewed by the client and form the basis for a discussion between the client and the team. After both parties have had an opportunity to exchange their thoughts, a formal Project Purpose must be drawn up by the consulting team.

The Project Purpose and the Deliverables. The Project Purpose must answer three questions—(a) what does the team intend to do and why? (b) How does the team intend to do it? and (c) What does the team intend to provide to the client? A good Project Purpose should do three things: First, it should define in specific terms the needs to be addressed, the issues to be resolved, and the importance to the client. Second, the Purpose should explain the general methods to be used in resolving the issues. And third, the Purpose should specify the intended outcomes, or *Deliverables.*

From the review and discussion of the client's needs, both the team and the client should arrive at a mutual agreement as to the specific needs that the team will address in the project. The needs should be clearly defined, and any issues that must be resolved to meet the client's needs should be identified. The reason for the project or the importance of the project to the client should also be explained.

For example, the Project Purpose might read as follows:

> The purpose of this project is to provide Ms. Susan Jones, the owner of the XYZ Company, with information that will enable her to determine how most effectively to make potential customers aware of the company's services. To do so, it will be necessary to determine the characteristics of the firm's potential customers—particularly with respect to their buying habits—and to review the potential media available for communicating information about the company. This information will enable Ms. Jones to develop a cost-effective advertising program that will secure additional customers for the company and increase the firm's revenues and profitability.

A good Project Purpose should be clear and concise. At the same time, it should leave no doubt in the reader's mind as to what is expected of the consulting team. The Project Purpose gives an overall definition and shape to the fieldwork experience. It must be understood by all those involved in the project.

The second element of the Project Purpose is a brief description of the general method the team intends to pursue to fulfill the Purpose and meet the client's needs. The team members should indicate the types of activities they are going to perform, the actions they intend to take on the client's behalf, and the procedures they will follow throughout the project. To continue with the example, the general method description for the above project might read,

> To provide Ms. Jones with the requested information, the team intends to conduct a survey of potential customers to obtain information on customer needs, perceptions of Ms. Jones's services, and the types of information media used by potential customers. In addition, the team will investigate alternative advertising and communications media for possible use by Ms. Jones. This will include information on the costs of various types of media, the effectiveness of each type, and the potential impact of each on Ms. Jones's business.

Finally, the Project Purpose should tell the client what to expect from the fieldwork: It should specify the Deliverables. What does the team intend to give to the client? In what general format? What information will be included? The client wants to know what he or she will receive at the conclusion of the project. The statement of purpose is the time to obtain agreement as to the Deliverables, because the successful presentation of the Deliverables means that the Project Purpose has been fulfilled. Deliverables can include analyses, charts, financial reports, market surveys, reviews of existing information, instructions on how to accomplish a task—almost anything that is within the scope of fieldwork and business consultation.

An example of the Deliverables for the project for Ms. Jones and the XYZ Company might be,

> At the conclusion of the project, the team will present Ms. Jones with the results of a survey of potential customers, in graphic and table form, that will explain the customers' needs, perceptions of the service, and buying decision process, including sources of information. In addition, the team will provide Ms. Jones

with a description of the alternative forms of advertising available within the XYZ Company's market area, including the costs of each number of exposures and the potential reach to the target customers. The team will perform a financial analysis of the various alternative forms of communication and provide recommendations for the media to be used based on cost-effectiveness of each type. Finally, the team will furnish Ms. Jones with a media plan, including advertising copy, artwork, and sample ads; dates and times for ad placement; and procedures for placing the ads with each media source.

Once the client and team agree on the Purpose and Scope of the Project and the Deliverables, a statement should be drawn up by the team and signed by both the consulting team and the client. This not only provides a basis for agreement and a definition as to what constitutes successful completion of the fieldwork; it also protects both parties' interests. The client has a means of evaluating the team's performance and determining if the project was done in a satisfactory manner. From the team's point of view, a clear Purpose allows the team to avoid having additional work requested by the client later in the project. Such requests tend to diminish the quality of the project by forcing team members to divert time and energy from the main purpose, thereby limiting the results.

The team should also make the client aware of certain other key items associated with the project by including in the statement of Project Purpose and the Deliverables a description of the following items.

• Any limitations that will be imposed due to limitations of time, funds, or resources.

• The approximate number of weekly hours the team is prepared to devote to the project.

• The recommended frequency of contact between the client and the team.

• Potential costs that may be incurred during the project that will be the client's responsibility. A pro forma budget for the project (see Table 3.1) should be produced and presented for the client's approval along with the Project Purpose.

TABLE 3.1   Sample Pro Forma Project Budget

Client: Weinzimmer Supply	
Project Manager: Chuck Fry	
Expenses	Est. Cost
Surveys: Printing Costs (350 @ .045 ea.)	$15.75
Long-distance phone calls	$45.00
Competitor research—mileage (225 miles @ .29/mile)	$65.25
Extra copies of final report (250 pages @ .045 ea.)	$11.25
TOTAL ESTIMATED COSTS	$137.25
Approved by: _____	

Developing a clear project scope and defining the Deliverables is a crucial step in the process. Remember, the team will be expected to live up to the agreement. Resist the tendency to try to do everything. Students generally want to do the best possible job for the client, and have a tendency to try to do too much in too little time. Be realistic in specifying the work that you will perform! In addition, take the time to define the project scope at the start of the project. It is not likely that you will establish the Deliverables at the first or second meeting with the client; sometimes, three or four sessions are needed before everyone is satisfied that the project is doable and that the quality of the output will be first-rate.

At the same time, you should try to establish the Deliverables as soon as possible. We have seen teams lose 4 weeks simply trying to determine what they need to do for the client; and once the time is lost, it can't be regained. The team then has to scramble to make up for the lost time, and quality generally suffers as a result. It is better to have a high-quality project that is narrowly defined than a poor-quality report that addresses several issues. Quality, not quantity, of the Deliverables is the crucial factor.

Conclusion. The importance of the assessment phase of the fieldwork process cannot be stressed enough. Prior preparation, careful analysis, attention to details, and a clear project are essential if the fieldwork experience is to be successful. All too often, consulting teams who do not take the time necessary to assess the client and his or her needs properly lose precious time at the start of the project trying to determine what the team needs to do. The lack of time leads to short deadlines, pressure, anxiety, and generally poor quality in the final outcome. It is absolutely essential that teams prepare for the project diligently, taking the time necessary and expending the effort required to get information. In addition, the team must seek to work together with the client to determine the client's needs and the Purpose and Scope of the Project to ensure that the client is satisfied.

THE IMPLEMENTATION PHASE

The second phase of the fieldwork process is the implementation phase. This is generally the most time-consuming part of the fieldwork experience. Having established the Project Purpose and the Deliverables, the student consulting team must now set about the work of satisfying the client's needs. The issues involved in implementation are numerous, and we will devote specific chapters to some of the more important ones, such as Information Gathering and managing the group process. In this section, we will highlight some of the more important issues involved in implementing the fieldwork process.

The key to successful implementation of the fieldwork is to develop a plan to address the client's needs and fulfill the Project Purpose, to communicate the plan to all members of the consulting team, and to manage the plan carefully throughout the fieldwork. Good project management and time management skills are important to the success of the project, as are dedication and effort from all members of the consulting team. Effective administration of the project depends on proper coordination and performance of a number of activities. Understanding what these activities are and how they fit together into the overall project experience is the first step toward effective management of the fieldwork.

ESTABLISHING OBJECTIVES

The first stage in the implementation phase is to establish specific Objectives for the fieldwork. The actual Objectives will differ from the overall Project Purpose. Objectives are more specific, tend to have a clear time frame, are often measurable, and must be attained in order to produce the desired results and fulfill the Project Purpose. Although Objectives are derived from the Purpose, Project Objectives are not the same as the Project Purpose.

Think of the difference in this way: The purpose of a football team is to win the game. The objective is to score more points than the opposing team. If the team attains its objective, it will fulfill its purpose. The focus of the team must be on the objectives, however, and on executing the game plan—both offensive and defensive—necessary to ensure that both objectives ("scoring more points" and "than the opponent") are attained. In addition, there may be specific objectives for individual players or units. For example, a defensive player may be assigned to "shadow" the opposing team's star player to ensure that that player does not have an opportunity to break free for an easy touchdown. Or, the offensive team may be assigned the objective of controlling the ball by executing a running attack and keeping the opposing team's offense off the field.

The fieldwork process is analogous to the football example. The Purpose of the consulting team is to address the client's needs by accomplishing some set of activities that will enable the client to do a better job of running his or her business.

The Objective may be to complete a market research study, perform an in-depth financial analysis, do a comparison between the client firm and competitors, develop a business plan, or any number of other similar assignments. If the team is successful in attaining the Project Objectives, it will achieve the desired result and fulfill the Purpose of the Project.

To attain these Objectives, other related Objectives may be assigned to individuals or subgroups within the team. If the team is made up of students from different fields of study, it is not uncommon for assignments to be made based on an individual's area of expertise. Thus, marketing majors tend to be assigned marketing surveys, accounting majors tend to be assigned financial analyses, and so on. This is part of effective group management and use of team resources, about which we will have more to say in the next chapter.

The essential point is for the team to break the Project Purpose down into a set of specific Objectives for the fieldwork. The actual Objectives will be based on the nature of the client and the case. However, there are a few characteristics that should be kept in mind when developing Objectives:

- *Objectives must be specific.* The more detailed, the better the Objective. People need to understand what is expected in order to be able to attain a goal. A general objective like "do a market survey" is not as good as one that might read, "Perform a survey of at least 120 potential customers in the defined market area via telephone to determine (a) if these individuals are aware of client's company, (b) the types of information used by customers in making a purchasing decision, and (c) the characteristics customers look for in deciding on a particular firm's products or services."

- *Objectives must be agreed upon by all members.* In particular, those individuals on the team who will have the primary responsibility for ensuring that the Objective is attained must be involved in developing the Objective and must take accountability for the outcome. Determining the specific Project Objectives is a group activity involving input and discussion from all members.

- *Objectives must have a clear time frame.* The expected date of completion for each of the key Objectives must be specified. Often, some parts of the project must be completed before others can be done: It is not possible to analyze data before it is collected! When activities have to be sequenced, it is important that the time frames be known by all the people involved and that everyone agrees that the time frames are reasonable. (Incidentally—it is our observation that most teams tend to be optimistic in estimating the time needed to complete the various elements of the project. Student teams generally indicate that they underestimate how much time the typical consulting project involves and as a result have difficulty in executing the project plan in an efficient manner. Be realistic in setting completion dates!)

- *Objectives must be realistic and attainable.* For Objectives to have any value in the management of the fieldwork process, team members must believe that they will be able to attain the desired goals. If Objectives are set too high or if the time frame is not adequate, the Objectives will have little motivational value. Team members will simply ignore the Objectives and will go about their activities in whatever manner they choose. This can lead to problems coordinating the fieldwork and can jeopardize the entire project. Good Objectives are aggressive, but are viewed by all team members as within the scope of their available time, resources, and efforts.

DEVELOPING THE ACTION
PLAN AND METHODOLOGY

Action Plans. The Objectives specify WHAT the team needs to accomplish in order to fulfill the Project Purpose. The Action Plan and Methodology indicate HOW the team intends to attain the Objectives. A good action plan defines—in detail—the specific activities and the steps that must be performed by team members if the Objectives are to be realized.

Action plans are organized according to the Objectives. For each Objective in the fieldwork project, the specific actions that need to be done to attain the Objective should be listed. Where possible, these should be listed in sequential or chronological order; that is, those activities that have to be done first are listed first in the action plan, and those activities that are dependent on successful completion of prior activities follow in order.

The members of the student consulting team should prioritize the Project Objectives and then discuss each of the action plans in turn. The basic rule to follow is to provide as much detail as possible in the action plan, while still allowing some room for judgment and flexibility. Do not have as an action plan, "Perform a market survey." Instead, break the action down into the logical steps that need to be done to complete the market survey. For example, if the Objective is to "Complete a telephone survey of the market," some specific action steps might include:

- Define the market area.

- Plan initial design of the survey; contact Professor Hill for assistance.

- Select the survey sample.

- Pilot the survey on a subsample of respondents.

- Revise and edit survey, based on pilot test.

- Administer the survey.

Once this Objective is attained, another Objective might follow, such as "Analyze survey data." Actions intended to attain this Objective might include such steps as:

- Enter survey results into data file.

- Analyze data via SPSS/PC, including:

  - Frequencies (all variables)

  - Cross-tabulations ("cross-tabs"; perceptual variables by demographic variables)

  - Correlations (perceptual variables with demographic variables)

- Produce frequency table.

- Produce cross-tab tables.

- Produce correlation matrix.

As can be seen from these examples, not every action is included in the action plan—only the key actions, those that are necessary to attain the Objective or that will contribute to fulfilling the Project Purpose. At the same time, the action plan is more detailed than simply stating vague generalities. It is important to give people a clear sense of what they are expected to do within the context of the project as a guide for action. Without a good action plan, the team will have problems coordinating activities, meeting deadlines, working together, and addressing the client's needs.

Making Time Lines and Meeting Deadlines. One technique that is beneficial in developing the action plan is to use a Project Management Chart such as the one shown in Figure 3.4. This is a sample chart, using the Objectives and action steps from the preceding examples. The chart lists the key Objectives and the individual action steps necessary for each Objective. In addition, the chart shows the intended completion dates and the person responsible for each action.

A project management chart such as this is very effective for project review and management. It also helps to clarify and outline the steps to be performed to fulfill the Project Purpose: By reviewing the project management chart, the team can determine what steps need to be done

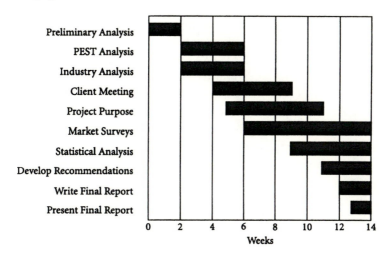

Figure 3.5. Project Management Chart

and the order or sequence of activities, and can ensure that all of the crucial activities have been included in the action plan.

By making and using a project management chart, the team members can ensure that they stay on course and make steady progress toward the project goals. It is important to make deadlines and keep them to ensure that the process proceeds smoothly. Deadlines should always be moved up at least 48 hours from the actual due date. Inevitably, things occur in the execution of the plan that were not anticipated during the development of the action plan. Computers and printers have technical problems, group members become ill or have other emergencies that must be attended to, clients cannot be reached for meetings, and more. Building a little space into the project schedule will ensure that any unexpected situations do not jeopardize the final result.

To make sure that deadlines are met, regular project management review meetings should be held. Team members should be required to report progress on their activities within the project action plan on at least a weekly basis, and a weekly meeting should be scheduled to review the overall status of the project. If individuals seem to be falling behind or if the actual time needed is longer than anticipated, the team can either adjust its activities to take the variation into account or can commit additional time and effort to get the project back on schedule. Such team discipline is essential for a successful project experience.

Conclusion. There is one other function that is served by producing a good action plan. Every client report should contain a thorough description of the methods used by the team to address the client's needs and to fulfill the Project Purpose. The Methodology should be described in sufficient detail that the project is *replicable;* that is, an outsider, if given the team's Methodology, should be able to replicate the team's efforts and would (theoretically) obtain the same results. By explaining the methods in such detail, the client is assured that the team's efforts were sufficient to yield the results and the client's confidence in the team's report is strengthened.

The fundamental point in this discussion is that the consulting team takes the time necessary to develop a thorough, detailed, and complete action plan. Trying to shortcut this process is a good way for the team to encounter difficulties later in the project. Many teams are tempted to plunge into the project, relying on a "seat of the pants" approach to completing the assignment. Experience with numerous teams and projects has convinced us that it is absolutely essential for the team to take sufficient time at the start of the project to develop a good plan of action to have a high-quality project.

PLAN EXECUTION

Key Issues in Plan Execution. Once the team has developed the action plan and the project management schedule, the team can set about the major business of the project: providing the client with the agreed-upon information and advice. The variety of projects that can be included within the scope of the fieldwork project is so broad that it is impossible to address all of the possible situations that a team will encounter in the course of a project. There are a few basic principles that team members should keep in mind, however, while carrying out their activities.

First, keep the client informed. Communication with the client is essential. The client wants to know how the team is doing and needs to know if the team is encountering any problems. Often, the client can assist the team by providing information or access to people and other resources that the team may need. However, the client cannot offer such aid unless the team is willing to keep the client informed as to the progress of the project. Teams should develop a regular routine of contact with the client, preferably at least weekly.

Second, adhere to the plan and project deadlines. Too many teams develop a plan and then forget about it shortly thereafter. It is a waste of time to produce an action plan and then ignore the plan in the execution. Good project management requires the discipline to adhere to the plan. Adjustments can be made as needed—and will be required during the execution of the plan—but adjustments should not negate the validity of the plan itself.

Third, work diligently and continuously. Many teams believe they can be "2-week wonders"—that is, the members will put off the project until there are 2 weeks to go and then attempt to pull the project together. Our experience has convinced us that nothing is further from the truth. Good, high-quality projects come from teams that manage the execution of the plan and constantly work to ensure they stay on schedule with the project. The fieldwork project often places a great responsibility on the consulting team. Clients will use the team's results to make decisions about their businesses, about commitment of their time or money, or even about their personal future. Such responsibility requires that the team act responsibly in the execution of its task.

Finally, a key issue in the successful execution of the project and the action plan will be the interpersonal dynamics among team members. This is such an important issue that we will devote an entire chapter (see Chapter 4) to discussing the group processes.

Controlling the Process. Good project management requires that the consulting team keep the process under control throughout the fieldwork experience. This does not mean that the team tries to dictate the process; effective consulting and fieldwork requires flexibility and adaptation. The process of working with a client, gathering information, working with a diverse group of team members, and the nature of the consulting relationship itself means that the team will constantly have to adapt to changing circumstances.

It is important, however, that the team remain focused on the Project Purpose and Objectives throughout the fieldwork experience. The team members must always keep in mind their responsibility to the client and must be willing to alter schedules and activities as necessary to attain the desired outcomes. Each member of the team should be committed to the client and to meeting the client's needs. This shared client orientation is very valuable in providing a common base for actions.

In addition, the team should establish Control Points. Control Points are periodic targets that must be accomplished en route to the overall Objective. For example, the team might break the project into component parts and specify that the various parts be completed by set dates. By setting up the proper Control Points, the team can be assured that it is making progress and can use these Control Points as a method of imposing additional discipline on the process.

PREPARING THE FINAL REPORT

The final outcome of the implementation phase is the team's final written report. In a way, the report is the culmination of the group's efforts, and it is therefore important that the report be done well. Teams should not allow a poor report to detract from their efforts and activities.

The primary standards for the written report should be that the report be PERFECT and PROFESSIONAL. The report should be edited and proofread at least twice before it is given to the client. Spellcheckers and other computer programs that assist with writing, such as grammar checks, should be used if the report is prepared on a word processing system. Poor grammar or spelling errors can indicate to the client that the report was prepared in a haphazard fashion and can lead the client to conclude that the content of the report is likewise flawed.

There is no universal format or length for student consulting projects; each project is unique. However, there are certain elements that should be included in the final written report:

• A letter of transmittal, in which the team formally presents the client with the report and thanks the client for allowing the student team to work with the client.

• A cover page, with the name of the client and of the members of the student team, at a minimum.

• An Executive Summary. The Executive Summary is NOT an introduction to the paper, nor is it a brief synopsis of the project. An executive summary is an abstract of the key ideas of the paper. It should contain a brief statement of the Project Purpose, a summary of the Methodology employed, summaries of the key findings and results from the team's research, and the key recommendations the team wishes to offer to the client. Many clients will not take time to read every page of the report, particularly if the project is a lengthy one; however, every client will read the executive summary virtually word for word.

• A table of contents.

• A statement of the Project Purpose.

• A brief history and background of the client organization.

• The environmental and firm analyses conducted by the team as preparation for the project.

• A detailed description of the Methodology employed by the team.

• The team's findings and results. Findings and results are a presentation of data; the facts that were obtained from research and investigations conducted by the team on the client's behalf and at the client's request.

• A discussion of the team's findings. The discussion should be used to comment on the findings—the importance of the findings to the client, the team member's attitudes regarding the findings, and so on. In addition, the team can use the findings section to combine information from various parts of the project and draw new conclusions that might be meaningful to the client. Finally, the discussion section should list alternative courses of action that can be considered by the client in deciding on a course of action.

• Recommendations. The recommendations should contain a detailed description of the proposed course of action and the specific methods and activities the client should use to implement the recommendations.

• Bibliography. A complete listing of all sources of information (including personal interviews and contacts, etc.) used by the team throughout the project.

• Exhibits/Figures/Tables/Appendices. Include supporting documentation that highlights, clarifies, or illustrates key points from the report. Any data obtained from research performed by the consulting team should be given to the client separately, in case the client wishes to do further research or analysis. These would include both raw data (survey forms, interviews, etc.) and any statistical data sets that may be included on a computer disk.

Conclusion. The implementation phase of the project is the most difficult part of the fieldwork experience. Most students who participate in the fieldwork process report that the project takes longer than expected and that the major difficulties that they encounter occur during this phase of the process. Careful preparation and planning, diligence in Plan Execution and project management, and careful attention to the preparation of the final consultants' report are absolutely essential if the team is to provide high-quality consultation and assistance to the client.

THE RESULTS PHASE

The results phase is the consummation of the fieldwork process. It gives the student consulting team an opportunity to impress the client with its efforts, and gives the client an important chance to exchange ideas with the consulting team to obtain information. Because it involves direct contact with the client, it is frequently a nerve-racking experience for the team. The team members have invested substantial time and effort in the project, and now the client will in effect evaluate the results of their efforts. This setting has the potential to create some tension and anxiety for the consultants.

There are two elements that must be addressed during this phase of the process: the presentation of the Deliverables and the Follow-Up Activities. The presentation of the Deliverables usually involves an oral presentation and time for discussion between the student consulting team and the client. Follow-Up Activities include client evaluation, team evaluation, and ongoing communication.

PRESENTATION OF THE DELIVERABLES

The presentation of the Deliverables occurs through an oral presentation of the major findings and recommendations of the team's Final Report. If the process has been carefully managed, the "Deliverables" are incorporated into the Project Objectives and have therefore been a central focus of the team's efforts. It should be kept in mind that the client's primary concern in the project is with the Deliverables—what did the team learn as a result of its investigations and research? What new information can the team provide the client that will help the client increase his or her firm's performance? What does the team suggest the client might do to improve the client's operations? These are the key issues and should be the focus of the team's presentation. The team should review the Project Purpose and the Deliverables prior to the final presentation to ensure that the presentation will satisfy the terms and agreement regarding the consulting project.

The Oral Presentation. The oral presentation is the final "formal" opportunity for the team and the client to meet together to discuss the project. If it is done properly, the oral presentation can enhance the report; if done poorly, the presentation can detract from an otherwise good project.

There are three keys to an effective oral presentation: practice, practice, and more practice. The team needs to take enough time to prepare the oral presentation. The presentation itself should be done by the one or two members of the team who are the most adept at public speaking. Every team member does not need to be involved in the formal presentation; however, every team member should be involved in the discussion with the client. The team member making the presentation may not be aware of all of the activities and information involved in the report, particularly if the project is a complex one that required the team to do a lot of independent research. In such cases, the presenter needs to rely on the individual team members to comment as needed and to respond to the client's specific questions by offering their own insights on the project.

The team should decide on the content of the Final Report and particularly on the types of visual aids that will be employed. The report itself should be rehearsed repeatedly until the delivery flows smoothly. It is wise to avoid the use of note cards or a detailed script: The presenter should appear professional and confident, in command of the information. Using detailed notes appears amateurish. The entire report should take no more than 30 minutes and should be contained on no more than two sheets of paper.

The visual aids to be used are especially important. Where possible, information should be given via graphs, charts, and similar pictorial methods. Avoid using visual aids that have long sentences or that are crowded with words; the client will start to read the visual aids instead of listening to the presenter. A bulleted format is much more appropriate. The visual aids should be timed to coincide with points in the presentation and should be handled by someone other than the presenter; this gives the presenter one less detail to worry about and allows full concentration on the presentation itself. If the team intends to use any special visual aids—computer graphics, video tapes, audio tapes—it is essential to double-check any equipment and, if possible, to have a backup system ready in case of system failure.

As with the project itself, the key is careful preparation combined with rehearsal and practice. Taking the time to prepare and to practice the presentation will increase the team's confidence and make the actual event appear polished and professional. If successful, the presentation can make a good project a great one.

Group Discussion. At the conclusion, the team should take time to discuss the project with the client. The client should be encouraged to ask questions. If possible, it is useful to give the client a copy of the final written report prior to the oral presentation. This gives the client a chance to review the material and have some questions prepared in advance.

The team members need to remember that they are the experts in this situation. They have been closely involved with the project for several weeks; the client has only had the regular team contact as a basis for information. The team members know what they have done, the efforts they have made, and the information they have gathered. Their job is to make sure the client is aware of the key findings and results and understands the team's recommendations. The client should be encouraged to ask questions of team members. Where possible, the team should prepare some questions for the client to encourage the discussion—questions such as: "Do these findings make sense to you?" "Are these results what you had expected?" "What do you see as the potential difficulties in implementing our recommendations?" Questions such as these encourage the client to share opinions and perceptions and give the team a basis for developing a response. The discussion provides a final face-to-face exchange between the client and the group and is an important part of the presentation process.

FOLLOW-UP ACTIVITIES

Many consulting teams assume that the fieldwork process is completed once the Final Report has been given to the client and the team has done the oral presentation of the Deliverables. Although it is true that many teams do not have further contact with the client, it is not true that the project has been completed. There are at least two formal actions that need to be taken: the client evaluation and the team evaluation. In addition, there may be a need for further communication with the client after the presentation of the Deliverables.

Client Evaluation. There should be a formal mechanism allowing the client to evaluate the project and the performance of the consulting team. This may involve a narrative summary, a rating form, discussions with the team or the project supervisor, or some combination of these evaluation mechanisms. The purpose of the evaluation is to provide the team members with feedback on their performance from the client's perspective. This information can give team members valuable insights into how they are perceived from the client's point of view, and can be a means of identifying areas that team members need to work on to improve their group interactions. Often, if a client has had sufficient experience with individual team members, an individual assessment can also be done and given to the individual team member as a means of self-improvement. The client evaluation is an important part of the fieldwork process. Because many students are having a "first experience" with this type of activity, the information provides them with insights that will help them to improve their personal skills and abilities.

Team Evaluation. At the conclusion of the project (if not throughout the project), team members should provide an assessment of individual team member's performance within the consulting team. The format of this assessment may vary. Some teams may prefer to do a written narrative, and others might prefer a structured rating form. The key point is to assess individuals' behaviors as members of the team. Often, team member evaluations are influenced by personalities—some people within the team may not get along with one another, and this tends to bias the evaluations. By focusing the performance appraisal on team members' actions and behaviors, some of this bias can be overcome. Behaviorally anchored rating scales (BARS) and similar formats are more appropriate in conducting this type of assessment.

It may be appropriate, however, for team members to provide feedback on certain personality dimensions. As we will discuss in the next chapter, much of the success of the fieldwork project is due to the dynamics of the consulting team. If people can learn to work together to accomplish a common purpose, if individuals are able to get along with one another in a work team setting, and if people can adjust to differences in personalities, it is easier to produce a high-quality project. On the other hand, interpersonal differences within a group can make the experience difficult and lead to poor results. Giving individuals feedback on how they are perceived by others in the team can be a useful source of personal information and a basis for self-improvement.

Ongoing Communication. Finally, there should be a formal mechanism to ensure ongoing communication with the client after the conclusion of the project. Often, teams make recommendations that the client will need to implement over many months. During this process, it can be very beneficial to the client to have access to various team members to obtain additional insights, opinions, assistance, or just to ask questions. It is not always possible to consider every possible circumstance that will arise in the course of implementing a team's recommendations. If the client can maintain some contact with team members, further help can be given, and the likelihood that the client will be able to implement the team's recommendations successfully improves significantly.

Team members should incorporate some mechanism or method of ongoing client communication within the Final Report. This may be as simple as including the phone numbers and addresses of team members as an appendix to the project report, or it may involve an agreement between the client and members of the team to meet together at some time in the future for further assistance. Whatever form the team may use, it is important that the team members bear in mind that their responsibility to the client does not end with the Final Report. When providing counsel or advice on matters that affect individual's lives or businesses, there is a greater responsibility to ensure that the client receives the best possible consultation and makes the right decisions.

CONCLUSION

The process of fieldwork consultation is rather complex. There can be literally hundreds of issues that need to be resolved or actions that need to be taken to ensure a positive experience and a high-quality result. Student consulting teams need to understand the fieldwork process and must be actively involved in the management of the process to satisfy the client. A well-managed process is crucial to the overall success of the project. In our experience working with student consulting teams, we have seem numerous examples of a well-managed team working with an "average" client and doing outstanding work. At the same time, we have seen many instances of potentially "good" cases and clients ruined by a team that does not control the fieldwork process. A commitment to understanding the nature of the client's needs, developing and executing a plan of action, and providing high-quality results is essential to maximizing the benefit of the consulting experience.

REFERENCES

Pearce, J. A., II, & Robinson, R. B., Jr. (1994). *Strategic management: Formulation, implementation, and control* (5th ed.). Burr Ridge, IL: Irwin.

Porter, M. E. (1980). *Competitive strategy: Techniques for analyzing industries and competitors.* New York: Free Press.

Thompson, A. R., Jr., & Strickland, H. A., III. (1995). *Strategic managment: Concepts and cases* (8th ed.). Chicago: Irwin.

4 | Managing the Student Consulting Team

Quick Tips

- Realize that student consulting teams are unlike any academic or social work group you have experienced before.
- The Project Manager's role in the group is to be a leader (but not the boss!) who schedules, coordinates, and completes administrative tasks. The Project Manager assumes responsibility for the overall project.
- The Task Managers assume responsibility for a specific task or activity.
- Team members play many roles, such as writer/editor, statistics or computer whiz, spokesperson, comedian, and grunt.
- Strive for mutual acceptance—each team member is entitled to her own perspective on the problem and should be valued for the contribution she brings to the team.
- Develop a set of common values that emphasize students' responsibilities to the client and to one another—motivation will naturally rise.
- Practice courtesy, trust, and cooperation toward your client and your team members. It will lead to higher team spirit and effective working relationships.

The purpose of this chapter is to offer some insights and information on the process of team management. It is clear from the many years we have spent working with student consulting teams that the single biggest variable that affects the quality of the final project is team dynamics—the interpersonal relationships among team members. Good teams produce good projects; bad teams produce bad projects.

Although many students will have some exposure to working together in teams from other courses they may have taken in their education, the nature of the fieldwork project makes the experience unlike anything most students have ever experienced. The amount of work and the intensity of the project (because the client is a real business person and not a textbook example) often leads people to behave differently than they have in other courses. We have seen roommates stop speaking to each other as a result of a fieldwork project! Other teams have had strong friendships develop out of the experience. Why do some groups succeed and actually enjoy the process while others come apart at the seams? In this chapter we will try to provide some insights and information on the dynamics of the student consulting team and give some suggestions on how to handle team management in an effective manner.

THE NATURE OF STUDENT CONSULTING TEAMS

Many students have had experience working with other students in groups or teams. More and more courses are incorporating some type of team or group experience into the instruction. Students may work in teams to solve problems, to analyze cases, to prepare class presentations, or as a learning exercise. Then, too, students are involved in any number of group or team activities outside the classroom. They may belong to a fraternity or sorority, participate on an intramural sports team, or belong to any of several campus organizations. Most students have been involved in many different types of groups and, as a result, they frequently assume that the fieldwork project team will be "just another team activity."

This is a false assumption. When we ask students to evaluate the consulting project experience, the one single area that they comment on more than any other is the team. Students generally say things like, "I didn't realize how difficult it would be to have to coordinate schedules with so many people," "It was hard to keep everyone motivated," "We had a lot of problems with a group member who didn't do his fair share of the work," or, "The best part of this experience was that I learned how to work with a group of different and diverse people." Even though the students had been involved in group activities, the unique demands of the fieldwork experience focuses attention on the group processes.

The student consulting team is different from many of the groups with which students are familiar. First of all, the student consulting team is a *task team;* that is, its purpose for being lies in the accomplishment of a single task, namely the fieldwork project. Once the task is completed, the team will disband and its members go off to their individual pursuits. Because students know that they are together for a relatively short time, they may not feel a need to try to develop any type of group cohesion. This can lead to difficulties in coordinating and managing the group processes.

Second, the consulting team is a *student team;* that is, it consists of people who are students in a college or university and are probably taking the fieldwork project for course credit. Their primary objective is to pass the course and continue their progress toward graduation. In addition, they are frequently taking other courses along with the fieldwork project. For the student, the project course may be important, but the demands of the project have to be balanced with the rest of the student's academic load. Furthermore, as students they cannot be "fired" or lose their "employment," as is the case for a professional consultant. Students are very busy people, and the fieldwork project offers little compensation other than a grade or the satisfaction of a job well done. All of these circumstances combine to make discipline and motivation of team members difficult.

Rhea, Management major:

"On discovering that the cases would be completed in teams of 3 to 4 persons, I soon felt uncomfortable because I have never really done well in a group atmosphere. This feeling soon disappeared with every class session and now I can honestly say that although I may still get nervous working in groups, I am sure that I will be more comfortable. The cooperation in the group was more than I expected. I now realize that group projects are not about competition with one another, but instead they are positive experiences

where work does not have to be the sole aspect in bringing individuals together as a team."

Third, student teams are frequently *cross-disciplinary teams;* that is,
they consist of individuals from a variety of functional disciplines,
who have diverse backgrounds. It is not uncommon for teams to have
marketing majors, finance majors, general management majors, accounting majors, computer majors, management science majors, engineering majors, personnel majors, or liberal arts majors combined
together on one team. In addition, the team members can represent a
diverse group of cultural and socioeconomic backgrounds. As a result,
the various members of the team bring their own unique perspectives to
the fieldwork experience—perspectives that may differ from those of
other members of the team. This can make communications difficult and
can lead to disagreements over various aspects of the fieldwork process.
Getting this group of individuals to function effectively as a team is a
significant challenge.
    Jim, Marketing major:

> "It was very interesting to work with other students with different
> opinions or approaches to the project. It was also a thrill to be
> considered the group's 'marketing expert.' "

Generally, the student consulting team is composed of individuals
with different personalities. Some students are more introspective and
prefer to work alone, while others are more extroverted and like the
interactions among group members. Some are analytical, preferring to
scrutinize data and information carefully, while others are intuitive and
have little regard for facts and figures. Some prefer to make decisions on
their own, while others prefer to discuss options with others. Some will
want to work independently, while others need direction and guidance.
The number of possibilities are as limitless as the differences in people.
This can create problems for the group, because not all personalities may
be compatible with others. Just as in most forms of human interaction,
team members don't always get along well with others, particularly those
who are different from themselves. Managing such a variety of people,
and getting them all to work together, is one of the major challenges that
the consulting team confronts.

Julianne, International Business major:

"One of my personal traits is that I like to work alone and be in total control. So I too had to learn to be more flexible in relating to my group and our client."

Finally, the consulting team is *externally focused;* this means that the team has a professional responsibility to an external constituent—the client—to provide the best possible information, advice, and consultation. Unlike other student teams that are concerned with a textbook case or an in-class assignment, the primary obligation of the team is not to the class or to a professor, but to a small-business person who is depending on the team for assistance with his or her business problems. This charge places a heavy burden on the team to maintain the client's trust and makes the team members accountable for their work in a manner that is unlike the classroom experience. If a student makes a bad decision or does a poor analysis in the classroom, the worst that will happen is that the student's grade can be affected. If a consulting team does a poor job and makes inappropriate recommendations, it can have a negative effect on the business and can cost the client personally. This "real-life" nature of the fieldwork experience increases the pressure on the student team members, which can affect their interactions with one another.

Because of these characteristics of the consulting team and the fieldwork experience, many students find themselves in an unfamiliar situation. For the first time, they are faced with the prospect of having to work together with a diverse group of individuals (some of whom they may find personally disagreeable), under a time deadline, with a project that may be bigger than any they have tackled in their academic experience, and with a serious obligation to address a client's needs. Students realize that there is very little in their previous education that has prepared them to function as professional consultants and that they will be learning as they proceed through the project.

Based on the experience of numerous teams with which we have had contact, there are some basic issues in team management that seem to increase a group's effectiveness. These are addressed in the following two sections. The final section in this chapter focuses on specific situations that lead to group conflict and how these situations can be addressed.

GROUP STRUCTURE AND ROLES

Even though the student consulting group is a team and relies on the cooperation and interaction of all members, there are some basic roles that need to be performed to ensure that the project is done properly. These roles lead to development of a basic structure for the consulting team that has proven to be effective in numerous situations. Bear in mind, though, that the structure arises out of the functions the group needs to perform. The members must still maintain proper respect for one another and must be committed to working together in a team environment for the group to be successful.

THE PROJECT MANAGER

The Project Manager (PM) has overall responsibility for the project and the team. In this role, the PM exercises the primary leadership role and is the central point of contact between the team, the client, and the fieldwork supervisor or course professor, and others involved in the project. The PM is responsible for the scheduling, coordination, and completion of all administrative activities. Ensuring that individual and group assignments are completed on time and in the proper manner is also the responsibility of the PM.

Accordingly, the PM might be thought of as the primary team leader. Yet the PM is also a member of the team! As team leader, the PM is still expected to carry a fair share of the team's workload. Many students assume that the PM is the "boss" of the team. This is a very inaccurate view of the PM's role. The PM assumes leadership of the team, but only at the behest of the team members. In most cases, the team is asked to select the PM prior to the Initial Meeting with the client. This serves to emphasize that the PM is responsible not only to the client and the project supervisor, but to the team members as well. The team will be relying on the PM to exercise effective interpersonal and administrative skills to ensure that the project is successful.

Some of the many duties and responsibilities of the PM are listed below:

• Provide any required administrative forms on time and on schedule.

• Keep a central file to store information pertinent to the project that is collected during the course of the team's activities.

• Delegate tasks to group members and coordinate group activities to ensure that workloads are balanced and tasks are completed according to the project schedule.

• Serve as the group representative at meetings between the group and other parties.

• Provide direction to group members about their various tasks, ensuring that each individual has enough resources and information to complete assigned tasks on time. At the same time, the PM is responsible for balancing workloads among team members to ensure equity among them.

• Ensure effective communications between the team and the client, between the team and the project supervisor, and among team members.

As can be seen from this partial listing, Project Manager is a position of significant responsibility within the consulting team. An effective PM must possess many skills. The PM should be a good communicator, both written and verbal, and be well respected for his or her abilities by fellow team members. The PM should exhibit a maturity of judgment and decision making that enables team members to develop trust in the PM's decisions and accept the leadership of the PM. A high level of self-discipline is another useful quality for a good PM, because team leadership requires that the individual be able to control his or her own activities and behaviors. Good interpersonal skills, such as empathy and understanding, are also useful qualities in the PM. And, of course, the PM needs to have personal integrity and the respect of the team members.

A good Project Manager not only manages to produce a high-quality project but does so by maximizing the experience for the team members. The best Project Managers are those who are coaches and enablers; that is, they constantly remind the team of its Purpose and of the responsibility of each member to the client and to one another, make sure that everyone knows their individual roles and responsibilities within the team framework, motivate the team to perform well, and assist people in achieving high levels of performance. If this is handled well by the designated individual, the Project Manager can enhance the fieldwork experience and secure a high-quality outcome. At the same time, we have seen a poor Project Manager devastate a team, from the standpoint of the team's performance on the project as well as in the relationships among the team members. Teams should be encouraged to select the Project Manager very carefully.

THE TASK MANAGERS

It should be clearly recognized by each member of a fieldwork consulting team that all members have the ultimate responsibility for producing a high-quality analysis and report. As part of the Action Plan and project management schedule, each team must determine the major tasks to be accomplished within the framework of the overall project. To make sure that each of these tasks is properly performed, a Task Manager should be designated for each of the major activities in the consulting project.

Recall from an earlier chapter that effective consultation involves the creation of a project management chart. Each of the major tasks on the project management chart should have an individual member of the group designated as its Task Manager—the person who assumes accountability for making sure that the activity is completed in a timely, accurate, and professional manner. Task Managers differ from the Project Manager only in the scope of responsibility. The Project Manager assumes responsibility for the overall project; the Task Manager assumes responsibility for a specific task or activity within the context of the overall project. Otherwise, the skills that each needs to possess—strong communication skills, effective interpersonal skills, dedication, maturity, and so on—are identical. Good project management depends on good task management. Effective management of the various activities can make the process go smoothly and contributes to the overall success of the field experience.

TEAM MEMBERS

Finally, we would be remiss if we did not say a few words about team members. Not everyone, by definition, will be a Project Manager, al-

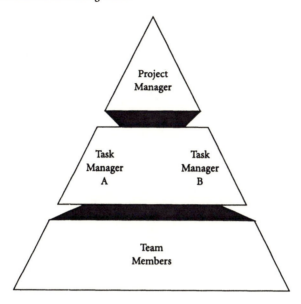

Figure 4.1. Consulting Team Organization Chart Group Member Roles

though everyone may have an opportunity to be a Task Manager. The critical variable in the group process is the degree to which the team members can get along with one another, put aside individual differences, and develop a cohesive team structure.

The team structure is more than the formal hierarchy of Project Manager-Task Manager-Team Member (see Figure 4.1). Team structure is about *the way in which team members work together.* The hierarchy ensures that the project and tasks get done in a timely manner. It is the team structure that determines how these get done—whether or not the experience will be enjoyable (or at least tolerable).

To have an effective team structure, teams should have a clear understanding of the *norms* that will guide individual and team behavior, and the *roles* that each team member is expected to perform. Norms are the shared values and beliefs of a group of people that shape their behaviors. Many teams quickly discover that the members share many common values and expectations. In such cases, the team develops a high degree of cohesion—not only are the individuals sharing the same team experience, they also share a common set of values. Teams that find they have shared norms find that they become friends through the field experience. They enjoy working together and develop mutual respect and trust among themselves that enables the team to function effectively. Of course, there is a down side to this situation. We have seen highly cohesive groups lose their focus on the project assignment. The people like each other so well that they tend to spend time together in non-productive ways. The best teams are those with a common focus on the project and a set of shared norms and values that enables them to work well together.

In addition, team members must have a clear understanding and respect for one another's roles. Roles are the behavioral expectations attached to a particular individual within the group context. In addition to the obvious roles of Project Manager and Task Manager, there are other, more informal roles that people frequently adopt within the context of the student team. These might include such roles as those listed here:

• *The Writer/Editor*—the person whose written communication skills are used to ensure that the project report is well written.

• *The Computer or Statistics Whiz*—the individual whose skills with a personal computer enable the group to develop professional reports, to analyze data, and more.

• *The Spokesperson*—the person whose verbal communication skills are so strong that the team expects this member to take the lead in presenting the report, talking to the client, and so on.

• *The Team Comedian*—the person who provides comic relief when the project gets intense, when pressure or stress builds, or deadlines get near, and keeps the team together.

• *The Grunt*—a very valuable person, the team member who always volunteers to help, stays at the word processor for long hours, is willing to go out for food, makes copies and cuts and pastes figures, and in general does all the jobs no one else wants to do but that need to be done right if the project is to be successful.

Of course, these are only a few of the many roles that individuals may take or develop within the project group; there are many more potential roles that can be performed within the field project. The key to a successful team process is for everyone to have a clear understanding of his or her role, for each individual to perform that role as expected, and for the roles to be harmonious. For example, the Team Comedian is useful at the right time; but at the wrong time, the Comedian becomes the "useless clown" whom others resent for failing to contribute in a meaningful way to the project. Good groups are those made up of people who share a set of common values and who understand what they are expected to do within the context of the team project to produce a successful result.

GROUP DEVELOPMENT AND GROUP DYNAMICS

It is also helpful for students to have an understanding of the process whereby a team develops into a working unit, and the dynamics that affect people when working within groups. Again, it should be kept in mind that the demands of field consulting and the characteristics of the field consulting process are often unlike anything that students have experienced in their lives or education. Consequently, the student consulting team will confront some issues within the group that will be unique. If students understand these intragroup processes, they may be better able to adjust and to work effectively, leading to a positive experience.

GROUP FORMATION

The first issue that the group will need to deal with is the process of group formation. In the initial stages of the project, the group members are getting to know one another and the client. In addition, group members have different backgrounds and experiences and team members are trying to adjust and to accommodate one another. There are a few key issues that the group should address in the formation process.

Mutual Acceptance. It is essential for student team members to keep in mind that the individuals on the team differ in terms of background. Many teams are established based upon a principle of cross-functionality—that is, the team consists of individuals with different major areas of study, such as accounting, marketing, management, or finance. If students haven't already discovered that people in different majors of a business program tend to view business problems differently, they will find out quickly that this is often the case. Accounting majors tend to look for figures and data; marketing majors want to understand the client's products and customers; and management majors want to study the interactions among people in the firm. Of course, this is a gross generalization: Certainly, in any team, students are bright enough to recognize the complex issues in a business situation. But each individual tends to view the organization through his or her frame of reference, and that frame will be greatly affected by the student's educational experience. As a result, different students have different frameworks, and this can lead to dissension among team members who "can't understand why you always want to look at the [accounting, marketing, management] issues."

Anthony, Accounting major:

"This was my last class before graduation, and I was taking all other courses in my major area. It was a challenge for me to take off my 'accountant's hat' and try really hard to see things from, say, a human resources or marketing perspective. But l know this will help me later in my career, since I need to learn how to interact with others who don't see the business problem in the same way I do."

Therefore, the first thing students should strive for is mutual acceptance—a shared realization on the part of the team members that each individual is entitled to his or her own perspective on the problem, and that each individual is valued for the contribution that that perspective brings to the team. One key to the successful formation and development of a team is for each member to make a commitment to accept the diversity in the team and even to value the diverse perspectives of team members. This mutual respect and acceptance does not mean that all members of a student team will be friends; it means that they are willing to put aside individual differences for the sake of the team. As one student put it: "I learned that you don't have to like each other to be able to produce some really good work. All you have to do is be willing to work together."

Communication. There is no way to say this enough: *Team members have to learn to communicate with one another.* Many of the problems teams have—both in project coordination and within the team—could be resolved or avoided completely if team members made a commitment to communicate with one another. In fact, it could be said that it is not possible to overcommunicate within the context of the team project. A note, phone message, meeting, whatever technique one uses—all are important to the ultimate success of the project and the team.

Team members need to communicate schedules, status of various tasks, expectations, intentions—the information need is substantial. Also, there is a lot of information associated with the team's field project. Client needs, firm and environmental analyses, market research, and the team's own investigative activities all add to the information load. As a result, it becomes essential that team members stress the need to communicate with one another. Effective communication is the cornerstone on which team processes are built. Cohesion, shared norms, and understanding of roles are all easier to develop if there is effective communication among team members.

Sandra, Economics major:

"Early on our team decided to make Monday afternoons at 5:00 our weekly 'check-in' time with each other. Even if there wasn't much new, we still called each other to see how things on the project were going. Having that time set aside let us know that we were in touch with each other and there to help solve problems each week."

Decision Making. Early in the process, the team should begin to determine how decisions will be made. Which decisions will be reserved for the Project Manager and which will be delegated to the Task Managers or team members? Will the decision process focus on individual decision making, on participation, or on consensus? How much information will be needed to make decisions? Who is responsible for the results of the various decisions that are made?

Keep in mind that there are literally hundreds of issues that must be decided in the course of the normal consulting project. Everything from who will write the various sections of the report to when to meet together requires a decision. It is useful for a team to establish a basic decision-making technique and then stick to this technique as much as possible. For example, if the Project Manager decides to use a consensus-based approach to decision making, then the team will need to meet often to resolve issues together.

Also, remember that individuals have different decision-making techniques. Some people prefer to make decisions intuitively and quickly, whereas others rely on facts and figures and are very careful in making choices. These differences in decision making can be another source of diversity among the team members and need to be considered when deciding on the structure of the project and the development of the group.

Motivation. Motivation is the force that leads people to take various actions. In the context of the student consulting team, motivation is a challenging task. Student team members are generally busy with other classes and assignments. Some are working full- or part-time as well as attending school. Many are seniors who are in the process of concluding their college careers and are seeking employment in business. And there are the usual social events that need attention, as well as personal relationships.

Add to this the fact that student consulting teams are generally working for course credit and the problem of motivation becomes more difficult. Between busy schedules and other demands on team members' time, the fact that students are essentially "volunteers" means that the threat of dismissal is not available. At the same time, aside from a grade there is no incentive for doing extra work. The result is that motivating team members to perform relies on peer pressure and developing a set of common values or norms that emphasizes the responsibility to the client and team. If people can share these basic orientations, then motivation is not a problem. If the team members do not have these beliefs, the group will be in for some difficulties.

Thus, the key to effective motivation of the student team is for the Project Manager to recognize the importance of a set of shared values that stress sacrifice, discipline, and responsibility to the client and to one another, and the importance of making sure that these values are instilled within the team. To do so, the Project Manager should make these values clear at the beginning of the consulting experience and should communicate the behavioral expectations that are based on these values— such as diligence, handing work in on time, cooperating with one another, and so on—to group members. In addition, the team should make clear at the outset that all of the members are relying on each other for a successful project. These peer expectations and the pressure that can be brought by the team on nonconforming members are powerful tools in motivating the consulting group.

Productivity. One of the important outcomes of the group is the final project report, and it is natural for groups to focus on completing this assignment as the key to the field experience. Yet focusing on the result can lead teams to miss an important point—that it is the process of producing the report that inevitably leads to the desired outcome. This *process orientation* is a key in determining the ultimate success of the team and the field experience.

A process orientation allows the team to address the issues of productivity: Are we accomplishing everything we need to do? Are we getting things done in a timely manner? How efficient are we? Are we wasting time or resources? If the team can address these issues, our experience indicates that the final result will be achieved and will be of high quality. It is the teams that lack this process view that inevitably run into difficulties as the members try to put together a project that will pass the course requirement but that may not fully address the client's needs. In addition, the team will probably find that the process will be less enjoyable if the focus is on the result. High-quality processes lead to high productivity and high-quality projects. To enhance the team's productivity, team members should concentrate on making sure that the process they use is effective and efficient, and that quality of process is at the heart of the team's efforts.

GROUP DYNAMICS

Group dynamics refers to the working relationships and activities among members of the student consulting group. In any group, the relationships among members are a key element in determining the overall performance and effectiveness of the group. Field consulting teams are no different. Team members and leaders need to recognize the importance of the group's relationships and must make an effort to manage these relationships.

Establishing Working Relationships. Team members should be sensitive to two types of working relationships that will be important in the field project: those with the client and those with team members. Time and effort need to be spent to build effective relationships to enhance the experience and to produce a high-quality result.

Perhaps the first rule of such relationships is an obvious one: Treat others with courtesy, honesty, and respect. It sounds trite or corny to say so, but the Golden Rule is still probably the best guide to developing effective working relationships—treat others as you would want to be treated. This means that team members are to be polite to one another and to the client. There is no need for rudeness or vulgar behavior. Common courtesy is essential. Team members should let others know if they have personal conflicts or schedule needs that will make them unavailable for some time period, and do so early in the process. Tell the client how often the team expects to be in contact and what the team needs from the client. Respect other members' needs and time, and the client's time. Be honest with one another and with the client. Maintaining high standards of behavior will help immeasurably in creating a team spirit and in developing effective working relationships.

Trust and Cooperation. The complexities of the typical field consulting project make it far too difficult for one individual to complete on his or her own. Thus, team members need to rely on one another to coordinate efforts to provide a successful result. This makes it essential that teams develop trust and cooperation among members.

There are three elements necessary for trust. First, team members must be *available*. Schedules need to be adjusted, when necessary, to facilitate meetings. Project and Task Managers must be able to locate team members and communicate with them on a timely basis. This means that team members need to be resolved to making themselves available as much as possible to the team and to one another.

The second element of trust is *accessibility*. This requires team members to be personally involved in the group's activities. When members attend group meetings, they must be willing to contribute effort. They need to share their ideas with one another and to learn to critique each other's ideas and efforts without offending. Many people are familiar with the phrase, "Criticize ideas, not people." This philosophy should guide the interchange of ideas within the student consulting team. It is absolutely essential that team members be able to access each others' ideas and thoughts to ensure the best results.

The final element of trust is *predictability*. Team members need to be able to predict each others' behavior. If people are predictable, they can be trusted because their behavior can be relied on. People who behave in an unpredictable manner—not showing up for team meetings, not completing assignments on time, and the like—cannot be trusted and can destroy the relationships among group members.

In addition to trust, student consulting teams need to have a spirit of *cooperation*. This means that individuals are willing to make personal sacrifices, if necessary, in order to allow the group to achieve desired results. Occasionally, it may be necessary to alter personal schedules to meet with other team members. Or, a team member with particular skills in some area such as personal computing may offer to assist others who are less adept. It is this sense of shared responsibility and a willingness to put aside personal desires for the sake of the team that fosters an esprit de corps among team members and builds cooperation.

Cooperation is essential, because the coordination of activities that is necessary to address a client's needs within the context of a field consulting project cannot be done without some degree of personal sacrifice and mutual support. Developing cooperation among team members is a crucial element of successful working relationships among members of consulting teams.

Matt, Finance major:

"Of our four-person team, three of us worked very hard and finished what it was we said we would finish. The fourth member was not around much. We couldn't get his material from him on time, and all he actually did was run a few numbers up for us and turned in three pages worth of stuff for the final report. That made me really mad. Although our report turned out OK and the client was satisfied, I am angry that we let him get away with it. I think if I am involved in a group project again I would handle it differently—but sometimes you are under pressure to finish things and it's just as easy to do it yourself. With the others, though, we all trusted each other and each of us came through in the end."

INTERGROUP CONFLICT

Any discussion of student team processes would be incomplete if we did not discuss some common problems that affect consulting groups. Even though each problem tends to be somewhat "situation specific," there are certain common themes in many group conflicts that need to be kept in mind by members of the consulting team. Some conflict and disagreement is inevitable in any team situation where different individuals are put together for the purpose of accomplishing a task. The type of conflict that teams should seek to avoid are those that can disrupt the team's processes and threaten the success of the project.

Role Conflict. One type of conflict situation occurs when there is a role conflict among team members. This typically results from two or more team members who want to perform the same role within the team. For example, some teams have difficulties because two members believe they should be Project Manager and there is a conflict over who is managing the team. Or, two people both try to exert control over a specific task or situation and disagree with one another about how best to perform the task. In such cases, conflict inevitably occurs as people disagree with one another.

To avoid role conflict, each member of the team must clearly understand the various roles and the expectations for each role. To do so, it is important to communicate with the team. If role conflict does occur, perhaps the best way to resolve the difference is to bring the situation to the attention of the team as a whole and permit the team to decide which person is best suited to occupy the role.

Lack of Motivation. Also sometimes known as the "free rider phenomenon," this is the problem that arises when one or two team members do not carry their fair share of the workload and thus create additional work for others on the team. One point to keep in mind at the outset is that free riders have to be addressed early in the process. It is not a good idea to wait and hope that, eventually, the free rider will "come around." Once the behavior pattern is established, it becomes progressively more and more difficult to get the person to give up the free ride and start to work.

Alicia, Accounting major:

"We knew we had to do something to get _____ back on track to do her work for the project. We probably waited too long—it was three weeks before the end of the class that we confronted her after talking with our professor, and we told her that if she didn't want us to 'fail' her on group evaluations, she would be in charge of editing and putting together the final report with material we would give her, and making a substantial part of the in-class and client presentation. We felt this was fair, since she had done almost nothing the whole time up to then."

Even more dangerous is the fact that a free rider can lead to additional problems within the group. Team members quickly begin to resent having to do more than their share of the work, which—if the resentment is allowed to grow—can cause other members to begin to slack off as well. We are aware of one situation where one free rider led two other members of a five-person team to follow suit, with the result that the remaining two members had to try to carry out the project on their own. As one might expect, the results were less than satisfactory.

In any case, team members will be asked to provide an evaluation of members' performance as part of the grading process. At times, this can be enough to encourage a free rider to alter his or her behavior. If not, active peer pressure is the next and best course of action. If the team members can agree to meet and present their concerns to the individual, they may be able to convince the free rider to become more involved in the team's activities. As a final recourse, the team can enlist the support of the faculty member who is overseeing the consulting project and ask the faculty member to confront the free rider. One point should be kept in mind about this problem. If a person really intends to "free ride" and is not concerned about his or her individual performance on the project, there is very little the consulting team can do. The nature of the project and of student teams means that team members cannot be forced or coerced to support the team's activities.

Other Team Problems. Some teams have difficulty developing effective working relationships due to the client's lack of cooperation. One student in a consulting team was told by a client that she "obviously hadn't learned anything in college," and that her work was "pretty useless." Another team was told by the client that, because their findings did not agree with what the client wanted to do, they hadn't done a good job in their research. One client refused to deal with two female members of a team and would only work with the three male team members.

Such incidents are clearly exceptions to the rule. In the overwhelming majority of the field experiences, clients are eager to work with the student team and are appreciative of the team's efforts. We have had clients take teams out to dinner or buy pizzas at the conclusion of a project. Another client regularly invites teams to his home, where he and his family prepare a home-cooked meal for the students as a way of thanking them for their efforts. Most clients fall between these extremes. They behave in a professional manner and expect the team to do the same. Nevertheless, there are some circumstances in which the client can cause problems for the team. In such cases, the team must keep in mind that—even if the client is wrong, rude, crude, and vulgar—a client is still a client and must be accorded the respect due to the client in a professional consulting relationship. Bad clients are not an excuse for bad team behavior.

One problem that can occur is the "Project Dictator" phenomenon. This occurs when the Project Manager becomes enamored with his or her authority and seeks to overmanage or control the team's activities. One team once remarked to a professor, "If you don't do something about her, we will." Naturally, such situations should be avoided. By choosing their own Project Manager, team members can make it clear that the PM serves at the pleasure of the team and can be removed if it appears that the PM is abusing the position. In any case, if team members will remember the previous comments on trust, cooperation, and effective working relationships, this problem can often be avoided.

One final problem that students should be aware of is the "Unassertive Member" issue. This person can often appear to be a free rider, but the issue really is that the person simply lacks assertiveness and is not much of a self-motivated person. If properly managed—that is, if given clear instructions and tasks and realistic objectives and deadlines—such people can be very effective and useful. The Unassertive Member's personal shyness can lead people to conclude that he or she doesn't care about the project when, in fact, that is not the case at all. With patience and support, such persons can make valuable contributions to the team's efforts.

CONCLUSION

Perhaps the most challenging aspect of the field experience is the management of the student consulting team. This is also the one variable that is arguably the most important in determining the overall quality of the work and the experience that the student consultants will have in the field project. There is no substitute for effective group management. Understanding a bit about the dynamics of the consulting team can help, but success requires people to be diligent in their efforts and sensitive to group dynamics. For further reading, we recommend Robert Bramson's *Coping With Difficult People* (1988).

An effective team can make the consulting project the highlight of a student's academic experience. A poor team can make the project a student's worst nightmare. We are constantly amazed at the ability of former students to recall—even after 10 or 15 years—their client for the consulting project. Many students develop friendships and personal bonds that last beyond the college years as a result of working together on the team. If properly handled, the student consulting team and the field experience can be very rewarding. All members of the team share a responsibility to one another and to their client to make the experience a positive one that they will remember fondly and that will enable each student to develop and grow in his or her education while helping the client to improve the client's business.

REFERENCE

Bramson, R. (1988). *Coping with difficult people.* New York: Dell.

5 | Launching the Fieldwork Information Search

Quick Tips

- Plan to gather both primary (original research collected by you) and secondary (published data collected by others) sources of information.
- Narrow and focus your search to determine what type of information you need. Use creative thinking techniques to broaden the range of ideas; withhold premature judgment about where to look for information.
- The annotated bibliography in Appendix C contains a representative selection of references—Internet addresses, books, periodicals, newsletters, and government agencies—from which you can begin to gather information.
- Primary data collection includes designing surveys, questionnaires, or interviews, and even some unintrusive, nonreactive measures for collecting relevant information.
- Adhere to the principles of question wording and the ethical guidelines when conducting primary research.
- Organize the information you collect according to its "light-shedding" ability, comprehensibility, and usefulness as supporting evidence in the Final Report.

The purpose of this chapter is to familiarize you with the process of gathering, organizing, and interpreting the information you need for forming alternative solutions and recommendations for your client. Remember, the quality of the information you collect is *only as good* as the quality of the questions you ask. First, the distinction is made between *primary* and *secondary* sources of information. Both will be valuable and often necessary for you to collect. Each plays a significant role in helping you diagnose and analyze business problems and issues. Once you have determined the type of data you presently need to collect, the decision must be made regarding what information is needed. (Unfortunately, this step is often abandoned in favor of the "let's go to the library and photocopy everything" approach to Information Gathering that is exhaustingly time-consuming and utterly worthless.) Once this decision has been made, it is appropriate to go to the library or other locations and find the information you require. We have created an annotated bibliography of selected references, Internet addresses, books, periodicals, newsletters, and government agencies that may be especially useful to students participating in field consulting. Organization of the information collected is the next step in this process, and it involves making careful decisions about what material is relevant to and suits the Purpose of the Project. Interpreting the information is a critical step in the research process, because it relies on students' abilities to develop sharpened skills as consumers of research. Understanding the value and contribution of both quantitative and qualitative information is discussed, and several pitfalls are presented. Students' successful progress through these steps in the information search facilitates the next activity in the consulting project, which is writing the Final Report and developing recommendations for the client business.

As summed up by one student consultant:

"Participating in the case, I obtained experience of the mechanics involved with the very beginning process of starting a business: market research, feasibility studies, and business planning. The amount of information available on a topic is incredible and abundant, if you just do a little creative thinking and digging."

PRIMARY AND SECONDARY
SOURCES OF INFORMATION

Background information on the client business and the environment in which it operates can be collected using both primary and secondary data sources. Specific kinds of information can be gathered from published information sources and records, which are called *secondary* sources. These include statistical summaries and information culled from databases and reference works such as *Standard & Poor's Industry Reports*. Simply put, information available from already published works, written by somebody else, is secondary. Data from *primary* sources, on the other hand, are information collected by students, usually at, but not limited to, the site of the client business or from customers, suppliers, and others who are directly connected to the business or its market. These can include quantitative information, such as performance behaviors or attitude surveys, pro forma statements, and break-even analyses; and qualitative information such as unstructured interviews conducted by students of the client, key employees in the business, customers, and so on. Most field consultants will collect both types of information, although there may be a focus on one or the other, depending on the nature of the problem or opportunity faced by the entrepreneur.

STEP 1: DECIDING WHAT INFORMATION IS NEEDED

With your problem diagnosis completed, you, your team, and your client have an agreed-upon idea about what you will be doing for the next several weeks. Now you must decide exactly what will help you make an informed analysis of this problem. First, it might help to do some creative thinking about the problem before you actually begin to dig up information. For example, consider asking yourself these questions:

• *What ideas can I think of that shed light on this problem?* Does the problem remind you of some image (e.g., a maze, a funnel, a tangled piece of string)? Metaphors and images can be very helpful in sharpening our "right-brain" (creative, flexible, playful) tendencies.

- *Who or what can tell me more about the problem?* Brainstorm and come up a with list of possible people to contact (within the university or college, friends or business contacts, family members of teammates, people in the business community, people in stores, associations, and meetings.

- *What would I (or the client) never do to solve this problem?* Other versions of this question are, "Who would never buy this product or service?" "Where would I never look for information to solve this problem?" This technique helps you reverse assumptions that you have made, by calling into question the way you are thinking about the problem. Here is an example: Arm & Hammer has sold baking soda in small yellow boxes for many years. As Charles "Chic" Thompson says in his book, *What a Great Idea* (1992), most people use one teaspoon of the stuff for every batch of cookies they make (and how often does the average person bake cookies—probably infrequently). So the box sits in the cupboard for months, maybe years, and Arm & Hammer doesn't sell that much of it. At company creativity sessions, A&H folks sat around and tried to come up with all the possible uses for baking soda that they could. Not surprisingly, there were many potential new uses for the product. After all, baking soda is a wonderful scent-neutralizer. So why not focus on its attributes of killing odors? Then it can be used in refrigerators, cat litter boxes, garbage cans . . . Ask, "To whom would we never sell baking soda?" One answer: babies. Response: "Aha—what about in diapers or diaper pails?" And creative solutions for how baking soda can be used in new ways and in new markets burst forth. Try this on your business problem. You just might come up with ideas that you didn't even know you had.

- Do not permit the use of "killer phrases" that stifle idea generation in this step of the information search. Symptoms include use of such comments as, "Oh, that will never work," "The client wouldn't go for it," or "I'm the marketing expert—that won't fly." Not to mention much more damaging phrases such as, "What a stupid idea!" Lighten up the group's atmosphere by suggesting that each team member is an appointed member of the "killer-phrase police," whose duty it is to call the group's attention to the use of a killer phrase—right when it is uttered. Awkward at the start . . . but it will lead to much more open communication, withholding of judgment until the appropriate time, and will absolutely free the group to come up with the most creative, worthwhile ideas (no matter how zany they appear at first) to solve the problem.

STEP 2: GATHERING INFORMATION

When the above questions have been discussed and answered, the consultants' next step is to gather the information. Secondary sources (see above definition) can be collected, read, and analyzed. Primary sources can be designed, collected, and analyzed. It is well worth it to take the activity of delegation to its art form in this step. Each team member can be responsible for specific types of information, divided as appropriate. First find out from each member whether she or he has experience with particular sources of data. Some students are very familiar with reference manuals, others with the Internet, and so on. This discussion will save the group needed time.

ANNOTATED BIBLIOGRAPHY
OF SECONDARY SOURCES

An annotated bibliography of secondary sources for your information search is provided in Appendix C. It is representative: That is, it is not a complete guide to all that is available pertinent to small businesses and entrepreneurship. We have selected works that may be especially useful for you to examine. You may find many others. The Bibliography is broken down into several categories: Reference Works (primarily works with broad coverage of businesses, industries, census information, etc., that are available in the reference section of most libraries); Internet addresses; Books (textbooks and trade books); Periodicals (both academic and practitioner oriented); Newsletters; and Government Agencies to contact for more information. You might want to start with Daniels's *Business Information Sources,* which is a most useful guide to reference sources in the library. The sources in the Bibliography have some intended audiences. We have attempted to provide a good mix of sources written for academic audiences including students, as well as sources written for entrepreneurs and business managers. You may want to gather materials intended for both groups, because this allows you to combine multiple perspectives.

PRIMARY SOURCES OF INFORMATION

Most field consulting cases will require you to collect some primary data based on your own observations of variables relevant to the business. In some cases, there is just not enough relevant secondary information to assist you in coming up with viable recommendations. As experienced by this student,

> "I looked for information in three libraries, and found only a two-page article that was useful. To get the information we were after, my group had to construct a survey and send it out to local businesses. We also got the address of an association for the industry and asked them for information. Even though the textbook maintained that the information may not be easily accessible, there is no way to fully appreciate that fact unless you have to search for the information."

There are some methods from which you may select the one (or two, or five) most suited to the needs of your project. Here is just a sampling of methods, along with suggestions for asking more effective questions.

SURVEYS AND QUESTIONNAIRES

Frequently, student teams design a survey or questionnaire to measure attitudes, opinions, or beliefs of individuals (such as potential or current customers). When designing such a *research instrument,* bear in mind that it is good to include some unstructured questions as well as structured ones. Unstructured questions are designed to capture qualitative information, such as reactions, interpretations, and feelings. Asking, "What do you like best about this product?" is one such question. This permits people completing your survey to tell you as much as they want to about the issue. You can also include some structured questions, such as "How would you classify the 'saltiness' of this cracker?" followed by a scale of responses that range from "very salty" to "not at all salty." Open-ended questions often bring you information that you couldn't possibly otherwise obtain, because you may not have thought to ask all the right questions. Surveys and questionnaires are often anonymous and confidential, thereby raising the likelihood that your information is

Table 5.1   Sample Survey

Dear Customer,
We are interested in finding out what you like or dislike about our products. Your preferences are important to us and will help us improve. Please circle your response. Thank you
very much for your time. Your completed survey may be presented for a free sample.

1. Do you eat baked sweets?		Y	N
2. If so, which ones? (e.g., cookies, brownies, etc.) _____			
3. Is the package attractive?		Y	N
4. If not, why not? _____			
5. Is it important, before buying, to see the product?		Y	N
6. Would you prefer a clear wrapper?		Y	N
7. Is the package color appealing?		Y	N
8. If not, what color would appeal to you? _____			
9. Would you notice this product on display?		Y	N
10. Could you identify the product on a store shelf easily?		Y	N
11. Did you know that the alcohol used is baked out?		Y	N
12. Would you buy this product for a child?		Y	N
13. If not, is it because of the alcohol flavoring?		Y	N
14. Would you like to see "No Alcohol" printed on the package?		Y	N
15. Do you find the selection of flavors adequate?		Y	N
16. What other flavors would you like? _____			
17. Do you think the product is of adequate size?		Y	N
18. If not, is it: **too big** or **too small**?			
19. Is the product's sweetness: not sweet enough?	just right?		too sweet?
20. Would you like to buy the product in larger quantities?		Y	N
21. If yes, how large?	3-5 6-10 11-15	16-20	
22. Would you purchase this product as a gift?		Y	N
23. Do you believe this is a high-quality product?		Y	N
24. How can the product be improved? _____			
25. How can the product's package be improved? _____			

THANK YOU FOR HELPING US TO SERVE YOU BETTER!

NOTE: The actual size of the survey has been reduced here. Y denotes "yes" and N denotes "no."

accurate and honest. Table 5.1 contains a sample survey developed by
a team of students for a gourmet sweet business. Notice the inclusion of
both short-answer and open-ended questions designed to probe the
customers' responses. This survey was distributed to customers at the point
of purchase in a retail establishment.

However, keep in mind that if your client is interested in distributing
a mailed questionnaire, the response time to expect is usually 3 to 5
weeks, with average response rates of 10%. If time is a critical considera-

tion, you may want to find alternate methods to collect your primary information.

As one student recalled,

"Once most of the employees learned that I was a student, they were more than willing to assist me in my research. If I had it to do all over again, I would suggest that we should just stick with phone surveys and forget about the mail."

INTERVIEWS

Interviewing subjects is a wonderful method to collect rich, highly detailed information that people can tell you one-on-one. Realize, however, that conducting interviews is more time-consuming than distributing surveys. It is therefore not realistic to expect to collect information from as many people by interviewing them as you could by surveying them. But, there are advantages for choosing the interview method. If interviews are conducted in person, you have the opportunity to observe the facial and body gestures of the subjects, which can often communicate much more to you than their words can tell. You are able to pursue and probe topics "off the main point" that might turn out to be very interesting and relevant.

If you do decide to conduct a personal interview, bring along a tape recorder. This allows you to ask probing and inquiring questions without worrying about writing everything down. Moreover, it also allows your consulting team and the client the opportunity to experience some of the interviewees' responses firsthand.

Interviews can also be conducted by telephone. Although you will certainly lose the rapport that is established with in-person interviews—as well as the observation of the individual—you can reach a geographically dispersed sample of people. Also, you can conduct more interviews by telephone than you can in person. If the information you are collecting is of a sensitive nature, the telephone affords more comfort to people because it is much less personal and you cannot see them.

Here are some guidelines for asking good questions on either surveys or interviews. Try to *avoid* the following:

- *Questions that are too long.* A rule of thumb is to ask no question that is longer than 20 words. Your subject will lose track of the question and you will only have to repeat it. On a survey, this type of question might even be skipped.

- *Confusing or ambiguous wording.* "Are you happy in your job?" is a useless question because it will mean so many different things to different people. For example, some may interpret that you are asking about their relationship to the owner or entrepreneur and whether it is satisfying; others will think you are asking about their opinion of the tasks they perform; still others will think about how much they like their co-workers when answering this question. Consequently, how can you come to any reliable conclusion about their responses when their frames of reference are so far apart?

- *Questions that rely on memory.* Don't ask people whether they liked a product or service long after the fact. Ask them immediately. Otherwise, people unintentionally distort what really happened (our recall ability is pretty dismal) and will give you inaccurate information. Better to have them record responses as they happen.

- *Surveys, questionnaires, or interviews that are too lengthy.* Even the most interested subjects will not have the time or patience to complete a set of questions that is too long. Keep questions to the point, and don't ask too much at once. You will be better off going back, or calling back, a second time to ask a few more questions than to overwhelm your subjects on the first round.

For more, and very sound, advice on the principles of question wording and other aspects of the research process, we highly recommend Uma Sekaran's book, *Research Methods for Managers,* listed in the Bibliography in Appendix C.

Finally, consider using nonreactive methods, so called because people are unaware that they are being "measured." For example, observe the number of customers that enter a store, which displays they visit, and their reactions to these displays. Observe the configuration in which employees sit at meetings, who talks first, who interrupts whom, and how frequently people speak. These nonreactive methods can yield very important information because they do not rely on the opinions, beliefs, attitudes, or biases of your subjects.

There is a plethora of methods for Information Gathering from which you can choose. Do read Appendix A on Ethical Considerations to be sure that the manner in which you collect information is not unethical or inappropriate.

STEP 3: ORGANIZING THE INFORMATION

The information search for both primary and secondary sources of data will no doubt yield much more than you can use or even need. The next juncture in the fieldwork process is to decide what information you will want to keep to analyze or explore further, and even what information you must go out and get that was not obtained in the first phase of data collection.

Information that is worth keeping is information that passes the "light-shedding" test. That is, this information should tell you something you didn't already know, should answer some aspects of the problem you are attempting to solve, and should do so in a manner that is understandable to all (most important, the client). Some guidelines for this step are provided below.

• Try to organize the information by prioritizing its value ("light-shedding" ability) to the client's problem.

• Combine quantitative and qualitative information to provide a more detailed analysis. For example, reporting that potential customers responded 4.5 on a scale of 1 to 5 regarding the product's taste is useful, but including remarks such as, "This cookie had a richer, moister, chocolate flavor than others I've tasted" really says much more.

• Be objective in the organization of information. Do not be infatuated with or wedded to a particular method or analysis. Just because you developed that snazzy survey with well-designed questions, does not mean that you should insist on it being used in its entirety in the Final Report.

- Use tables, charts, figures, and other graphic material liberally in the Final Report. They are often easier to understand than paragraphs chock full of statistics.

- Use media that are available to you, including tape recorders, video cameras, and slides. They can convey material in a concise and vivid manner.

- The information that your consulting team decides to "discard" can be sent to the client as an attachment to the Final Report. This prevents your efforts to collect it from being wasted. In addition, information that you deem irrelevant now may be just what the client needs several months (or years) from now.

- Be familiar with the information that has been collected by the team and how it can be used as supporting evidence for the conclusions made in your Final Report.

STEP 4: INTERPRETING THE INFORMATION

One of the greatest benefits of this entire information search process that is at the heart of fieldwork is that it helps you become a more knowledgeable consumer of research. Just as pieces of a puzzle each contribute to the "picture," so too does information educate you incrementally about the underlying problem. However, be wary of several pitfalls that exist in this step.

- *Avoid making unwarranted projections or conclusions based on data analysis.* Be sure you can support each and every conclusion or prediction you make. Cite the numbers or statistics or responses that led you to the prediction. If a leap in logic is required, watch out. This is not meant to undervalue the contributions of intuition and "gut reactions" to the study of the problem. In fact, you will want to include these, too—just say that they are intuitively based or are best guesses.

- *Avoid being overly critical and "shooting down" ideas before their merits have been discussed.* Some of the most useful recommendations sound off-the-wall when they are first proposed, before anyone has the chance to reveal the unexpected opportunity they present. To defend your ideas from being shot down, defend all ideas from being shot down. You will not be viewed as so self-serving then.

• *Avoid favoring certain types of information over others* just because you are more comfortable with them. We have previously discussed the values of quantitative, qualitative, and nonreactive methods, and although we may accept this intellectually, when push comes to shove in the heat of team discussions we may be reluctant to accept information that we are not used to. Some team members prefer a "Just the facts, ma'am" approach to interpreting information. Other members will want to look beyond the facts for meaning. Both preferences are valuable—and necessary for completing an effective project.

• *Avoid engaging in "mind-guarding"* to distort, bury, or otherwise eliminate from the analysis and discussion any negative or unfavorable information that might upset the group or the client. In one field case, the students were interviewing current customers about the services provided by the client (at the client's request). Lo and behold, some of the responses they received were less than complimentary to the client. Needless to say, the students were very concerned about how to present such obviously negative information. One solution: Present it confidentially and in aggregate. Translation: Report only the average scores of the customer group as a whole, or, if open-ended questions are used, the major themes that came up in the narrative responses. In this way, no customer could be identified by the use of peculiar wording. It would have been poor consulting to withhold this information from the client. Successful entrepreneurs and business managers are often prepared to receive the bad news with the good. After all, it is only the bad news that sometimes spurs much needed changes and improvements. Good news can sometimes lead to complacency ("Things are going well, the customers like us, so why do anything differently?"), which is deadly in the current uncertain business environment.

Realize that this process of collecting and interpreting data and information for your client is fraught with problems. Here are just a few things for you to ponder:

• How much information is enough? You want to avoid overload and analysis paralysis, but don't err on the side of too little data, either. A sample of 10 customers, for example, might not be adequate as a base for conclusions.

• Use of intuition versus number crunching: Don't underestimate the value of your hunches and gut feelings about something. Just make sure your report mentions that these are not based on data, but on experience and intuition.

• Factor in the strategy of the firm, its life cycle stage, and trends such as cyclicality, seasonality, and other issues that affect your analysis.

• Don't try to impress the client with sophisticated analyses that he or she cannot understand or use. Find out just what level of sophistication the client expects and stick with it. Nothing is more useless to a businessperson than data that cannot be interpreted and a report that goes on the shelf because it is not understandable.

• Understand the difference between raw data and useful information, and the role of judgment in the analysis process. Your client is "paying" for judgment as much as, or perhaps more than, raw data. Go beyond the numbers and turn them into meaningful recommendations, suggestions, and conclusions.

Now that the information has been gathered, organized, and interpreted, the student consulting team has what is required to begin that final phase of fieldwork: writing the Final Report and making recommendations to the client.

REFERENCE

Thompson, C. (1992). *What a great idea*. New York: HarperCollins.

6 | Developing Recommendations and the Final Client Presentation

---

Quick Tips

- The Final Report and recommendations are the most important phase of fieldwork, for these suggest to the client what is to be done.
- Combine information from several sources, interpret data, and include team members' intuition and feelings in the project.
- Consider that each piece of your research should shed light on this question: "What does this suggest the client should do?"
- The more ideas your team can generate, the better the probability of coming up with recommendations that will be creative and valuable to the client.
- Develop a set of alternatives and list the opportunities and obstacles associated with each, using your information base as evidence to support them. Doing this in chart form for each alternative action provides a clear, concise guide for the client.
- The more precise the team is in its recommendations, the greater the chance that the client will be able to adopt and execute the suggested actions.
- Tell the client exactly what to do, and in what order. Specify actions and their sequence. Identify persons responsible for actions and any sources of assistance.

- Become familiar with technical writing styles and incorporate figures, diagrams, and pictures. Remember, the recommendations are the key to fieldwork success.

L et's assume that you have done your research, gathered your data, and have been reasonably successful in managing your group processes. You are now ready to prepare the Final Report and recommendations and to present your results to the client. The project is about to come to a conclusion.

But hold on! In their eagerness to wrap up the project and finish the fieldwork, many consulting teams neglect to pay proper attention to the most important phase of the fieldwork process—the recommendations. This is understandable, for most of the time has been spent in the assessment and implementation phase of the fieldwork process. But don't overlook the critical importance of this final element of the experience.

In fact, from the client's point of view, this is the central issue of the whole project: What should the client do? As far as the client is concerned, this is the key element of the process. When the client comes to the team for assistance, it is generally because the client wanted some information or advice that would assist in improving the operations of the client's business. The client is looking to the consulting team for suggestions or recommended actions that will resolve the client's problems and concerns. Thus, the development of good, clear, understandable recommendations is the most important element in the fieldwork project.

Based on our experience and interviews with numerous clients, there are four major reasons clients do not adopt or accept the consulting team's findings and recommendations:

- The client does not believe the recommendations are consistent with the firm's problems or with the team's information and analysis.

- The client accepts the legitimacy of the recommendations but does not understand how to go about implementing the recommendations due to a lack of detail in the team's proposal.

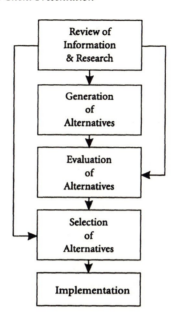

Figure 6.1. Developing Recommendations: A Decision-Making Model

• The recommendations are too theoretical or unrealistic. The team presents general statements or concepts without specifying what the client should do, or proposes a course of action the client cannot perform due to lack of funds or resources.

• The client is unwilling to accept the team's recommendations because the recommendations are not what the client expected or are inconsistent with the client's preconceived ideas of what should be done.

In these situations, the actions suggested by the consulting team do not bear upon the client's needs or activities, and the value of the project—from the client's point of view—is questionable. However, there are actions that the team can take that will avoid or alleviate these situations.

To avoid the scenario of doing all the consulting work and failing to have a positive impact on the client's organization, this chapter will discuss methods for developing solutions and recommendations for the client. A decision-making model for the fieldwork experience has been developed as a framework for the chapter and is shown in Figure 6.1. The model will form the basis for this chapter's discussion of the methods to be used by consulting teams when preparing recommendations for the client.

REVIEW OF INFORMATION AND RESEARCH

The first step in developing recommendations for the client is for the team members to review the results of their Information Gathering and research about the client and the client's needs. This should be a comprehensive review of all information gathered in the project. Everything from the environmental analysis to the discussions with the client to the results of the team's own research should be brought into review.

In the process of reviewing the information, the team should bear in mind that the purpose is to develop recommendations for the client that address the client's needs as specified in the team's agreement concerning the scope of the project and the Deliverables. Much of the information the team has gathered, though useful and interesting, may not be of much value in developing recommendations about the client's particular problem or situation. Thus, the first thing the team should do is filter out or screen the database and identify the information that bears upon the client's needs.

This does not mean that the team should ignore any general research or information. Frequently, the best or most creative recommendations come about because someone on the team gains an insight from some bit of information that was obtained early in the process and that appeared to be only tangential to the Purpose of the Project. For example, in one project a team member recalled that in the initial stage of gathering information on the industry it was observed that customers reported obtaining information on a client's services from an article in a local newspaper. The team was able to recommend the client incorporate the article into advertising literature for the local market area, thus saving the client time and money in developing an effective promotional campaign.

Thus, one of the objectives of the team in conducting the review of the information base should be to synthesize information from all phases of the project. The team should look for common themes or concepts, similarities in ideas, or bits of information that may be related to the client's specific need. Time should be taken to do some brainstorming or creative exercises to maximize the chances of developing original, effective, and imaginative solutions and recommendations.

Another goal for the information review is to incorporate the results of the team's own research efforts into the overall database. Teams often do product reviews, customer and market analyses, competitive assessments, or other types of primary research about a specific market area that applies to the client's business operations. The information that the team gathers from its own efforts should be incorporated into the general information that the team obtains from its review of secondary data sources.

To perform the review, the team should meet together and discuss the information. It is helpful to take notes on the discussions as a basis for future activities. The team should remember that the purpose of the review and discussion is to make recommendations to the client, and should focus attention on those items of information that appear to have the most importance from the client's point of view. Effort should be made to tie information from the entire project to key points and ideas that can be used to generate alternative recommendations or to help decide between alternatives. The team should make a list of these key points, to be used as a reference for the team and the client. If possible, these key findings should be shared with the client prior to actually generating alternative recommendations to be sure that the client is in agreement with the data.

In addition, the team should perform a final analysis of the project information. This would include combining information from several data points into key findings; interpreting subjective data; and incorporating "soft" data, such as team members' intuition and feelings, into the project. Many times, teams cannot identify a specific piece of information that has led to a conclusion or recommendation. Instead, the team has an overall impression or insight that certain issues may be important. It is important to include these in the analysis; many of the most crucial pieces of information that lead to successful business decisions come from a willingness of managers to trust a hunch or go with their "gut feeling" about a particular situation. These feelings cannot always be articulated, but are the result of intensive study and experience. Naturally, the student consulting team should be careful about trusting such "soft" information, particularly because the members probably lack any in-depth expertise in the client's area of business. But caution does not mean that the team should overlook such insights.

The key question—from both the team's and the client's perspective—is, "What does this suggest the client should do?" Each piece of information or research analysis is potentially useful in suggesting a possible course of action for the client. The team needs to remember that the goal is action—things the client can actively do to influence his or her firm in a positive manner. Information that cannot be translated into client actions may be interesting to the client, but it has very little value.

GENERATION OF ALTERNATIVES

The second phase of the process of developing recommendations is for the team members to generate alternative recommendations, courses of action, or solutions. This is an exercise in creativity and in brainstorming. The team members should meet together after the review of information and after they have had some time to consider the implications of the information base. At this meeting, they should generate a list of potential actions for the client. One member of the team should be appointed to keep track of the opportunities by taking notes and writing down every idea that the team can generate.

It is important that during this phase of the recommendation process the team members NOT criticize or critique the ideas. No one should say "that's not workable," or "that's a stupid idea" during this meeting. Ideas that may appear to be far-fetched or unrealistic can lead to new ideas that are creative and that can yield high results for the client. Imagination tempered by a sense of the client's needs and the situation can produce new insights that may suggest a new course of action for the client. If team members immediately start to evaluate ideas and offer criticism, the thought process will be stifled and the team will not develop many new ideas.

During the alternative generation phase, team members should try to develop as many ideas as possible, with as many variations as possible. For instance, one alternative may be to increase sales through a new advertising program. Within this alternative, there may be several variations, such as ads on radio, in television, newspapers, telephone books, billboards, flyers, and so on. The team should strive to get as many options as possible out on the table for consideration. Variations are important, because these will give the team a choice in deciding on the best course of action for the client.

Also, the team should be certain to include negative options in its deliberations. These might include "do nothing—maintain the status quo," "close down the business," or "sell off the enterprise and do something else." Team members sometimes feel that they must give the client alternative solutions that are consistent with what they believe the client wants to hear. This is unprofessional consulting. The team has a responsibility to give the client the best advice and recommendations possible, even if the client may not want to hear these alternatives. Therefore, the team should be sure to consider all options in the generation of alternatives.

The essential point to keep in mind: The more ideas the team can generate, the better the probability of coming up with recommendations that will be creative and valuable to the client. To have the best chance of generating ideas, avoid criticism. Consider every suggestion. Use "wild" ideas to generate new recommendations that are more workable. And include negative options in team discussions.

EVALUATION OF ALTERNATIVES

Once the team members have developed the list of ideas, they are ready to begin to evaluate and assess the various alternatives. Some ideas can be ruled out very quickly—perhaps because an idea is too expensive for the client to afford, or because the client cannot acquire the necessary resources, or maybe the idea is just too bizarre to have any real merit. As long as these ideas can be used to develop additional alternatives, there is nothing wrong with ruling out certain options. But do not eliminate an option out of hand; with a few modifications, the idea may be workable. For example, a client may not be able to afford a large advertising campaign to increase market share. But perhaps there are other, less expensive ways for the client to generate awareness. One student team found that a client in the health care industry could not afford the expense of advertising on television. Instead, they suggested the client develop a relationship with a local television station and provide the station with weekly "Health Updates" to be presented on the local evening news broadcast as a service to viewers. The station was pleased to have this "free" service from a local health care expert and the client received regular weekly publicity that led to a significant increase in sales. It is important to use constraints as sources of creativity, not as obstacles to ideas.

To evaluate the alternatives properly, the team members should analyze the pros and cons of each alternative in light of their information base and research. It is helpful to specify a set of minimum criteria for alternatives. For example, the team may specify that no alternative can cost more than some fixed amount that the client is willing to budget for the concept. Another criterion might be that the alternative must satisfy some minimum condition in the environment, such as "must be consistent with the community's needs" or "cannot decrease area employment." Or, the team may develop a client-based criterion, such as "must result in at least three new accounts" or "cannot exceed the current physical space available at the client's location." These minimum standards, or "hurdles," can be used to eliminate some alternatives fairly quickly, allowing the team to focus on the remaining options.

Once the team has developed the set of potential alternatives, the next step is to assess the pros and cons of the various options. Teams should develop cost-benefit analyses for some alternatives and determine the net value of the recommendation to the client. Alternatively, the team may list the "opportunities" and "obstacles" for each of the alternatives, based on the environmental assessment and the team's research and analysis. Another approach is to list the "advantages" and "disadvantages" of each option. Whichever technique the team chooses, it is essential to tie the evaluation to the information base. Remember that one of the reasons clients do not adopt team recommendations is that the client believes that the suggestion is not consistent with the team's analyses. Don't make this mistake! Be sure that you can justify your evaluation on the basis of your information.

Where possible, the team should create a series of charts that list each option and the pros and cons of each on a single sheet of paper for comparison purposes. Such assessment forms make valuable additions to the Final Report and are wonderful guides to writing up the evaluation of alternatives and recommendations for the client. As with any chart, such assessment forms should be simple. Use key words or phrases only: Don't write out all your arguments and reasons. Another useful technique is to make two columns, one labeled "Advantages" (or "Pros") and the other labeled "Disadvantages" (or "Cons"), and to list the various reasons in the appropriate columns. Whatever form the team may choose, the main point is to provide a clear and concise assessment of each of the potential alternative actions.

SELECTION OF ALTERNATIVES

Now it is time to choose—what should the client do? The team must now commit to a course or courses of action and convince the client that these recommendations will be of the greatest benefit to his or her business. This is the crux of the entire project. As far as the client is concerned, this is the reason for using the student consulting team. It is essential that the team make good decisions.

Before selecting one or more alternatives from among the set of options the team has developed, the team should first develop a set of decision criteria. These criteria should be based on the client's needs and capabilities and on the team's information base and research. It is hard to remain objective at this point in the fieldwork process—the team members have probably been living with the project for at least 2 to 4 months and are often very immersed in the situation. Nonetheless, they must bear in mind that the client expects the most objective assessment and recommendations possible. The team members must now make a conscious effort to avoid personal biases and perspectives and must take an impartial attitude toward the project. Therefore, it is useful for them to "take a step back" from the project and attempt, objectively and rationally, to develop a clear set of criteria that will guide the selection process.

Criteria may include such issues as costs ("Cost cannot exceed $500"), timing ("Must be able to complete work by December 31"), and other physical limitations ("Cannot hire any more personnel"). Other standards may include client-imposed limitations ("Needs to be able to work out of client's home") or key client needs ("Must have good probability of increasing sales at least $10,000"). Additional selection criteria may be based on the team's assessment of the environment and a determination of any standards imposed by the market or competitive situation, as well as any information uncovered by the team members through their research ("Price must be no more than $15," "Must have a minimum size of at least 5,000 square feet," "Maintain consistency with surrounding landscape," etc.). The key decision criteria should be listed and distributed to all members of the team prior to the meeting to select the recommended course of action.

At this meeting, the team members should discuss each of the remaining alternatives in light of the decision criteria. Financial analyses such as cost-benefit assessments should be completed before the team meets for deliberation. The members should review the options and, through discussion, seek to identify the course of action that appears to offer the best overall result for the client, given the criteria and the team's objective and subjective evaluations.

This is not an action to be taken lightly. As one student put it,

"When you're telling a client what to do, you realize this is real money and real people's lives that you're talking about, not just some case study. It's a little intimidating to realize that someone is going to spend a substantial amount of his or her money and invest their time and effort because of something you told them to do."

The responsibility of the consulting team to the client is substantial. The team members should discuss the options carefully and completely to ensure that the best decision results from their efforts.

IMPLEMENTATION

All too often, team members think that once they have made the recommendation, their responsibility ends. "From here on out, it's in the client's hands" is an all-too-often heard refrain. This is an inaccurate and unprofessional attitude. The selection of an alternative or alternatives does not end the team's obligation to assist the client by providing a thorough report. In fact, selecting the alternative is only the beginning of the work!

Remember that the second reason that a client often fails to use a team's suggestions is that the client does not know how to implement the recommendations. The client agrees that the team's suggestion makes sense and is consistent with the information available. The client may even congratulate the team for its efforts and compliment the members on the thoroughness of their investigations. But if the client takes the report and files it in a cabinet, never to be seen or read or used again, the team's efforts have been essentially wasted. The client has received no benefit from the experience.

To avoid this situation, the team needs to give great care and attention to developing the implementation steps for the chosen actions. There are two key points that must be satisfied: First, be sure that the team explains precisely how the recommended course of action meets the decision criteria and fits with the information base and analyses. Second, the team must "walk the client through" the actual implementation of the proposed course of action.

CONSISTENCY

The first thing for the team to do is to make sure that the client understands that the course of action is consistent with the team's information and research. Care needs to be taken in explaining how the actions tie in to earlier sections of the report. Where possible, the team should cite specific evidence or findings as part of the justification for the recommendation so that the client can see the connection between the suggestion and the research.

In addition—and it sounds a little ridiculous to say this, but we have seen teams overlook it—be sure to tell the client how the solution addresses the client's need or problem. Connect the solution to the letter of agreement and the Deliverables. Make sure the client understands that "this is what you asked the team to do—here is how this action fulfills your request." Don't assume that the client will obviously see that the team's suggestion is the only logical choice. The team must explain its reasoning to the client.

STEP-BY-STEP INSTRUCTIONS

The second important issue for the team is to explain to the client precisely how to go about implementing the recommendations. It is not enough to tell the client what action the team suggests. The team must tell the client what to do, when to do it, how to do it, who should do it, and where to do it. We cannot emphasize this enough: *Every good recommendation includes a detailed implementation plan.*

Teams often overlook this important issue. The team has been working on the project for an extended period of time and tends to develop blinders; that is, the team has a tendency to assume that the client knows what the team is thinking because "after all, it's the client's business." Remember that if the client knew what to do, he or she probably would not have sought the assistance of a consulting team! The client is relying on the team to help as much as possible with the actual implementation of the team's recommendations. Teams that fail to do so are not meeting the client's needs and are not fulfilling their professional obligation to the client.

The "Cookbook" Approach. In making recommendations to the client, teams should take a "cookbook" approach to the solution. Think of a typical cookbook. A person has a need—to prepare some food dish for eating. A good recipe or cookbook "walks" the reader through the cooking process through a series of step-by-step instructions that, if followed, will result in the finished product.

Making recommendations to a client should use the same approach as the cookbook or recipe. The client has a need. The team believes that it has the "recipe" that offers a solution to the client's need. Now the team must take the client through the steps necessary to reach the desired result.

All too often, we have seen teams make recommendations like "Improve manufacturing operations," "Develop more effective advertising," or "Try to lower costs of service." Then there follows a series of platitudes that read like something out of a textbook, with little regard for the client's specific situation. Consulting problems are not easily resolved with generic or textbook answers. Instead, solutions must be tailored or "custom fitted" to the client's needs and circumstances. Telling a client to "develop more effective advertising" and then offering some prepackaged comments is like writing a recipe that says "Bake a cake. Combine flour, eggs, milk, and sugar in a bowl and pour in a pan and put in an oven." Avoid making this error.

Instead, the team needs to describe to the client the specific action steps the client should follow to implement the recommended solution successfully. This means telling the client precisely what to do and in what order. It means specifying how actions are to be done and their sequence. It means identifying the person or persons responsible and the people that need to be contacted for assistance. In short, tell the client exactly what to do, in what sequence (when), how, and by whom. The more precise the team is in its recommendations, the greater the chance that the client will be able to adopt and execute the suggested actions.

Technical Writing. Team members should become familiar with technical writing styles. Teams often tend to write in an informal style; perhaps at some point in their education, team members were told to "write the way you speak." When it comes to technical writing, this is not very good advice. Most of us speak in a verbal shorthand or use poor grammar in conversation. In addition, when speaking we have the advantage of the entire communication context, including nonverbal messages, gestures, intonation, and so on. This is absent from the written word, which requires more precision in structure in order to convey the desired message.

As an example, consider a simple act such as tying one's shoelaces. Imagine writing a set of instructions that could be read by a person that would explain precisely how to tie the laces on a pair of shoes correctly. Anyone who has ever tried to do this realizes how difficult technical writing can be. Or, consider many manuals that come with personal computers. It is difficult to explain to a reader the actions that have to be done to operate the computer successfully; as a result, many companies include "tutorials" that actually take the reader through a step-by-step process to develop hands-on experience with the computer or software.

Now imagine writing a set of instructions for a client that tells the client how to reduce manufacturing costs by improving the plant layout, eliminating inventory, and combining work stations. Or, try to envision a set of instructions telling a client how to develop an ad and place the ad in a local newspaper. The steps are very complex and difficult, and a good deal of precision is required in writing to be able to convey clearly what needs to be done.

One technique that teams should use is to take advantage of pictures, figures, and diagrams. The old saying, "A picture is worth a thousand words," is still true. Effective illustrations can help guide a client through the process and give the client a "map" that can be followed to ensure that the desired result is obtained. We have seen students develop diagrams of a plant layout, placing machines and offices in the proper locations. Other teams have produced sample advertisements for the client and have even copied the ad into the suggested format, such as a newspaper layout or Yellow Pages directory. Teams have made sample radio commercials for clients and given their clients a cassette tape to use as a model.

The use of illustrations does not excuse the team from the necessity of employing precision in writing the implementation instructions. One technique we have used when in doubt is the "roommate" approach. Have a member of the team read the implementation instructions to a friend or roommate who is not associated with the project. Then, ask the person to explain what has to be done to carry out the instructions just read. If the person can explain the steps with reasonable precision, the team should be fairly confident that the client will be able to do the same. However, the basic rule is that the ability to follow the instructions and implement the solution is the TEAM'S responsibility, not the client's. If the client cannot implement the recommendations because the client does not understand what needs to be done, the fault lies with the consulting team.

CONCLUSION

Perhaps no aspect of the fieldwork experience is as overlooked by teams as the need to present viable, clear, precise recommendations and the appropriate implementation steps necessary to put the recommendations into action. Yet no element of the fieldwork is as important as this is—for if the client does nothing as a result of the team's efforts, then the project has been an academic exercise and nothing more. The team has a professional responsibility to the client to make recommendations that are consistent with the information and research the team has conducted, and to provide the client with specific instructions as to how best to implement the team's recommendations. It makes little sense for team members to go through the fieldwork process only to fail in the final stage. Team members should adopt an attitude early in the process that says, "The recommendations are the key. Let's make sure that everything we do is pointed toward making good, clear, understandable recommendations that our client will be able to implement."

A FINAL WORD

By now you are well on your way through the fieldwork experience, and you probably agree that it has been (or is turning out to be) an experience like none you have had before. Has it been worth it? Like countless other students before you, no doubt you had moments when you questioned why you were doing this. But, in our many years of supervising field projects and talking with hundreds, maybe thousands, of students who have traveled down the path, we have seen students come back and recount tales of fieldwork days. Students brag about the valuable lessons in business leadership, management, conflict resolution, group dynamics, continuous improvement, and many other areas that fieldwork taught them, and how the "real" world didn't seem so strange at all when they entered full-time employment or began careers after completing fieldwork.

Congratulations! You have survived fieldwork and know more about how a business operates than you could possibly have learned from a textbook case. You also were probably privy to the agonies and ecstasies that come with business ownership and management, including the indecisiveness, the crises, and the uncertainty of tomorrow that confront any businessperson in the 1990s. Your self-confidence is surely stronger, because you successfully enacted the role of consultant and contributed meaningfully to someone's livelihood and future. One of our students put it simply yet eloquently by saying,

"This project taught me more than all of my other business classes combined through four years of college."

Whether your experience is quite so profound remains to be seen. Even if it does not seem so yet, there is still tremendous benefit for those who engage in fieldwork. So make of it the most you can by giving it your best effort, and take from it all the experience and wisdom offered by your client. There is something to be learned by everyone, and it is waiting for you.

Professionalism, Confidentiality, and Ethical Considerations of Fieldwork

Appendix A addresses some of the more sensitive issues that are part of the fieldwork experience. As representatives of their university or college, students enter the business community to assist local entrepreneurs or business managers and to widen their learning horizon as students. In the course of doing so, they may encounter questionable exchanges or practices, inappropriate requests, or may themselves unintentionally commit unethical actions.

Although most professors and case coordinators undoubtedly encourage students to inform them if such issues arise, some students may feel uncomfortable about bringing up such information, or uncertain about how to handle the situation. This section provides a set of guidelines and suggestions that should help students become aware before hand about what they might encounter during field consulting.

• Treat the client with respect, and consider all discussion of the case with the client and the team members to be proprietary and confidential, not to be revealed to outsiders (this includes other classmates, friends, and even family), unless so permitted by the client. If you are conducting fieldwork that is sponsored by the Small Business Institute, the SBI program guarantees that all information about the client and his or her business will remain confidential.

• If the client's request seems inappropriate to you, do not wait and hope that it will eventually be resolved. Speak up early! Seek your professor or case coordinator immediately if he or she is not aware of the situation. We stress the use of the word *seems* here, because if a student feels uncomfortable about a request, then she or he deserves to have it clarified. If it turns out that the student's reaction was unjustified, so be it. At least the request is now better understood by all parties. Inappropriate requests can include things like being asked to conceal your identity as a student when collecting information (thereby "duping" others); being asked to "pretend" to be a potential customer, all the while collecting information from an unsuspecting competitor; being asked to "make up" data to support a request for external funding; and certainly includes all incidents that would be covered under most academic sexual harassment policies. Students are not powerless; call attention to these situations early.

• Students should not use the names, collected data, pictures, or anything else of client businesses for publicity purposes. If you are involved in fieldwork that is particularly relevant to the university's mission (developing a business plan for a not-for-profit business that helps unemployed people start home businesses, for example), ask for the client's (written) permission to notify university staff or the school newspaper. Publicity may be beneficial and the client may like it, but always ask first.

• If you discover that the client is engaged in unethical or illegal business practices, report the matter to your professor or SBI Director. This individual will use his or her best judgment about how to deal with the problem.

• It is considered unethical for students to hold a vested interest in companies that maintain business relationships with their client. So if your uncle is the supplier of widgets to your client, it is best to avoid consulting with that client.

• Do not accept gifts from a client, nor give gifts to the client. (Yes, this even includes university souvenirs such as pens, mugs, and sweatshirts.)

• Students should not be hired by the client as members of the firm while the fieldwork is taking place. After the fieldwork has ended, students are free to accept such employment arrangements if they are offered.

• If any activity, conversation, or incident "feels" to you to be unethical or unprofessional in nature, seek the advice of your professor, case coordinator, or SBI Director.

APPENDIX B

The Role of the SBA/SBI in Fieldwork

One of the more common forms of fieldwork experience is the Small Business Institute (SBI) program of the U.S. Small Business Administration (SBA). The SBI is both sponsored and funded by the SBA as part of the Administration's efforts to provide small business assistance. Each regional office of the SBA (see Chapter 5) is responsible for the SBI programs within its geographic area, and provides support to the colleges and universities that administer the SBI program.

The SBI program is operated as a community service by area colleges and universities. The program may be "housed" in the College of Business or in a specific department; or, it may be associated with a Small Business Development Center or similar form of community outreach. Wherever its location, the basic operations of the SBI are similar.

AUTHORS' NOTE: As this book went to press, the future of the SBI program was highly uncertain due to cutbacks in government appropriations.

Each college or university is given a grant by the SBA to provide consulting services for a specific number of cases. A "case" is generally an individual small business in the local area. The institution that operates the SBI program agrees to provide assistance and consultation to the business about some problem or need of the firm. In exchange for the service, the SBA agrees to pay the institution a fixed sum to help defray the costs of providing the consultation. As of 1995, the SBI program provided sufficient funding to allow its member institutions to offer services to more than 6,000 small business clients per year!

Once a particular college or university is accepted into the SBI program by the SBA, the institution designates an individual as the SBI Director. The SBI Director is responsible for managing the program within the institution and for maintaining a relationship with the regional and district SBA office. To help support these individuals, there is a national organization of SBI directors called SBIDA (Small Business Institute Directors Association) that provides regular information about the SBI program and holds regional and national conferences annually to enable the SBI program continually to improve its performance. Generally, the SBI Director is a faculty member at the college or university that provides the SBI program.

The SBI program is often incorporated into the fieldwork experience course at the host institution. Whether the title is "Fieldwork Experience," "Business Consulting," "Small Business Strategy," or "Senior Project," the common denominator is the support of the SBA for the consulting effort. If your college or university is one that incorporates the SBI program into the fieldwork experience, you should be aware that—in addition to the issues we've covered in previous chapters—you will also be expected to perform certain administrative functions in support of the SBI program.

Like most programs that are supported by the federal government, the SBI has certain requirements for reporting that must be met by the consulting team. In addition to providing a written Final Report and an oral report to the client, you will find that your team must keep track of the time spent on the team's activities, because these hours must be reported to the SBA periodically throughout the fieldwork experience. In addition, your team will be expected to record all expenses associated with the fieldwork project and to keep written records or receipts for all funds expended. You will also be required to have the client sign a form acknowledging receipt of the Final Report and indicating acceptance of the team's efforts. These represent the minimum reporting and administrative requirements; there may be additional requirements, depending on your institution or the nature of the SBI project. Check with your SBI Director for additional information.

The legal requirement for reporting of information should not be taken lightly! Your team is working under a government grant, which makes you a government contractor and a representative of the SBA as well as of your college or university. Poor or sloppy reporting can cause problems in handling a case with the SBA and can cause your institution to have its case allotment adjusted accordingly. In addition, there are various legal (as well as ethical) issues that pertain to the reporting of information to the federal government and its agencies. You should take care to administer your relations with the SBI and the SBA in a professional manner. This is almost as important as your relationship to your client!

There are some advantages you may enjoy in the fieldwork experience as a result of the SBA/SBI relationship. One is the added degree of professionalism and the experience you acquire from dealing with a government agency. Many students will find very quickly that the influence of the government in business activities is quite pervasive. The SBI program offers some insight into the nature of working with the federal government. As a representative of the SBI program, you will also find that you have a certain stature that clients will often accord the student team. Clients are generally told that the students are part of a government program, and this "legitimation" can enable you to develop a strong and professional relation with the client early in the fieldwork experience.

An additional advantage is the ability of the team to gain access to the large information and knowledge base about fieldwork projects provided by SBIDA. The Small Business Institute Directors Association has developed student manuals that provide detailed information and examples for the fieldwork project and help "coach" the team through the process. In addition, SBIDA has several databases of information that can be used as a resource. Check with your SBI Director for access to these materials.

Often, students involved in the SBI program will interact with other small business support organizations, such as a Small Business Development Center (SBDC), the Service Corps of Retired Executives (SCORE), a local Technology Incubator, the Chamber of Commerce, and similar types of agencies. Not only are these potential sources of information and assistance, but working with these agencies gives you additional opportunities to learn more about small business in the area and provides a chance to meet and to network with people who have a wealth of knowledge and experience about managing a business.

Certainly, successful fieldwork does not require that the student consulting team be involved with a formal program like the SBI. However, the advantages of the program and the opportunity to work with the SBA as a partner in providing assistance to small businesses add to the overall fieldwork experience. You should make every effort to gain from the program and to use the program to your benefit.

APPENDIX C

Annotated Bibliography
of Secondary Sources

Appendix C provides an annotated bibliography of secondary sources for your information search. It is representative; that is, it is not a complete guide to all that is available pertinent to small business and entrepreneurship.

REFERENCES

The sources listed below are just some of the information available in your academic or public library. Some are very general, providing industry-level data or demographic statistics; others are more focused on entrepreneurship and small business.

INDUSTRY SOURCES

Standard industrial classification manual. Washington, DC: Government Printing Office.
Reference guide that breaks industries into S.I.C. (standard industrial classification) codes for government statistical purposes.

Standard & Poor's industry surveys. New York: Standard & Poor's.
Covers major domestic industries. Provides basic analysis, cites trends, and gives historical perspective. Provides current analysis, tracks latest developments, and gives appraisals of investment outlook.

Thomas Register of American manufacturers. New York: Thomas Publishing.
Thomas Register catalog file. New York: Thomas Publishing.
List products and services alphabetically, contain company profiles and a product index.

U.S. industrial outlook. Washington, DC: U.S. Department of Commerce, International Trade Administration.
Contains industry reviews and forecasts with tables and charts. Gives international trade forecasts.

DEMOGRAPHIC SOURCES

Survey of Buying Power Demographics USA. Sales and Marketing Management Magazine.
Geographically organized demographic information geared for business use.

Sourcebook of demographics and buying power for every zip code in the U.S. C.A.C.I.
Contains residential and business demographic information.

ENTREPRENEURSHIP AND SMALL BUSINESS SOURCES

Bangs, David H., Jr., is the author of the *Planning Guide Series.* All volumes are published by Upstart, in Dover, NH. The series includes:

- *The business planning guide: Creating a plan for success in your own business* (6th ed.).
- *The market planning guide: Creating a plan to successfully market your business products or service* (3rd ed.).
- *Managing by the numbers: Financial essentials for the growing business.*
- *The personnel planning guide: Successful management of your most important asset* (3rd ed.).
- *The start-up guide: A one-year plan for entrepreneurs* (2nd ed.).
- *The cash flow control guide: Methods to understand and control the small business' number one problem* (2nd ed.).

Baty, G. B. (1990). *Entrepreneurship for the nineties.* Englewood Cliffs, NJ: Prentice Hall.
A very readable, useful guide written for the would-be entrepreneur, for the growth-oriented business. Topics cover everything from what kind of company should be started to financing (the care and feeding of bankers is just a sample) to marketing and running the show. Baty has run three venture-capital financed companies, sat on 20 boards, taught entrepreneurship, and advised government on entrepreneurial and technology issues.

Cohen, W. A. (1990). *The entrepreneur and small business problem solver.* New York: John Wiley.
An encyclopedic reference to starting and growing a small business, this work is full of resources and answers to frequently asked questions in financing, marketing, and managing the business. Appendices of directories and organizations make this a useful tool.

Daniels, L. M. (1995). *Business information sources* (3rd ed.). Berkeley: University of California Press.
One of the most useful guides to reference sources in the library. Organized by topic, including national and international statistical sources, this annotated bibliography includes a section on entrepreneurship and small business, with a subsection on functional areas within small business, such as sources on marketing the small business or on human resource policies in small business.

Dible, D. M. (1986). *Up your own organization!: A handbook for today's entrepreneur.* Reston, VA: Reston Publishing.
This book takes entrepreneurs through the three-step process of business creation: recognizing and evaluating personal needs and abilities; preparing a plan for attaining your goal; and acquiring the financial resources necessary to make the plan a reality. Best of all, the book includes several appendices with names, addresses, and phone numbers of venture capital companies and associations, small business investment companies, and checklists galore.

Encyclopedia of associations. (1995). (29th ed.). Detroit, MI: Gale.
A manual of all trade and industrial associations.

Gladstone, D. J. (1988). *Venture capital handbook.* Englewood Cliffs, NJ: Prentice Hall.
A guide to the entire process of preparing a venture capital (V.C.) proposal and raising venture capital, written by a venture capitalist who has reviewed thousands of proposals. The point of view is the entrepreneur who approaches a V.C. firm.

Lasser, J. K. (Lasser Tax Institute). (1989). *How to run a small business.* New York: McGraw-Hill.
A popular guide written for new and established entrepreneurs. Useful for students doing location planning or analysis, developing accounting and recordkeeping systems, and related financial matters.

McGarty, T. P. (1989). *Business plans that win venture capital.* New York: John Wiley.
A helpful resource for students completing a business plan for their fieldwork project. Each component of the plan is covered in detail, with sample business plans provided.

National Foundation for Women Business Owners. (1992). *Women-owned businesses: The new economic force.* Washington, DC: Author.
The NFWBO is the source of statistics and information on women business owners. Combined census and NFWBO/cognetics data are presented, along with case studies profiling successful women entrepreneurs.

O'Hara, P. D. (1990). *The total business plan: How to write, rewrite, and revise.* New York: John Wiley.
A guide to business planning and business plans, with "how to" tips for researching sources and presenting the plan to others.

Pinson, L., & Jinnett, J., are authors of the *Small Business Basics* series, published by Upstart in Dover, NH, which includes the following books.

- *The home-based entrepreneur: The complete guide to working at home!* (2nd ed.).
- *Anatomy of a business plan: A step-by-step guide to starting smart, building the business, and securing your future* (2nd ed.).
- *Keeping the books: Basic recordkeeping and accounting for the small business* (2nd ed.).

Small business sourcebook (annual). Detroit: Gale.

One-stop shopping for fieldwork projects. Part 1 of this two-volume guide describes sources and services for more than 200 small businesses, complete with relevant associations, periodicals, reference works, trade shows, and more. Part 2 contains general organizations and publications for small business, including universities, government agencies, and venture capital firms.

Timmons, J. A. (1990). *New venture creation.* Homewood, IL: Irwin.

This well-regarded work guides students through the process of starting a business from scratch, with many examples, case studies, and hands-on experiences as guides.

Vesper, K. H. (1993). *New venture mechanics.* Englewood Cliffs, NJ: Prentice Hall.

This book covers the nuts and bolts of entrepreneurship with many examples drawn from real businesses to illustrate the points. The focus is on the implementation of strategy in entrepreneurships, including refining, developing, protecting, and implementing ideas. A sample business is included in an appendix.

Welsch, H. P. (1996). *International entrepreneurship and small business bibliography.* Chicago: International Council for Small Business.

One of the most recently published bibliographies on small business and entrepreneurship sources, it is organized by topic (franchising, marketing & promotion, taxes, etc.) and also by country, for works that focus on a particular nation or culture. Full citations are provided. It is a very handy reference tool.

ABSTRACTS AND INDEXES

Business Periodicals Index

ABI/Inform

Predicasts F&S Index

Wall Street Journal Index

Lexis/Nexis

BOOK REVIEWS

Mangelsdorf, Martha E. (1994, April). In search of the small-business. *INC.*, pp. 37-48.
Mangelsdorf's top three books for the small business start-up process are:

- Merrill, R. E., & Sedgwick, H. D. (1993). *The new venture handbook: Everything you need to know to start and run your own business* (rev. ed.). New York: AMACOM/American Management Association.
- Kirk, R. W. (1993). *When Friday isn't payday: A complete guide to starting, running—and surviving in—a very small business.* New York: Warner Books.
- Lonier, T. (1994). *Working solo: The real guide to freedom and financial success with your own business.* New Paltz, NY: Portico Press.

INTERNET SOURCES

As of January 6, 1995, Jerome Katz had compiled more than 200 internet addresses containing resources for entrepreneurs in EGOPHER: The SLU Entrepreneurship Gopher. They include the following:

- EGOPHER "Top 10 List" for Entrepreneurs

- EGOPHER "Top 10 List" for Entrepreneurship Academics

- EGOPHER "Top 10 List" for Entrepreneurship Students

- YAHOO

- SBAOnline

- Internet Entrepreneur Guide

- Entrepreneur's Guide to Small Business Information—Library of Congress

- Internet Resources for Small Business

- Family Business Bibliography—Kennesaw State

- Financial Assistance From U.S. Small Business Administration Current Business Statistics

- INFORMATION ON COMPANIES, ORGANIZATIONS AND INDIVIDUALS—Tillman

- BBG #4: Sources of Information About U.S. Companies

- BBG #5: Industry Information Sources

- BBG #8: International Business—Researching the Foreign Market BBG #IS: Market Data Sources

- Service Corps of Retired Executives (SBA Online)

- Local SBA Offices (SBA Online)

- Small Business Institutes (SBA Online)

- Women's Business Ownership (SBA Online)

- Basic Guide to Exporting

Additional Internet addresses include:

- .misc entrepreneurial discussions

- .entrepreneurs on operating a business

RESEARCH METHODS

The following works are useful sources for research methods and techniques, including problem identification, survey or questionnaire design, methods of observation, and so on.

Sekaran, U. (1984). *Research methods for managers.* New York: John Wiley.
This book cover the entire research process, with a focus on applied (e.g., business and social science) settings. Great chapters on data collection (e.g., conducting a structured vs. unstructured interview), and preparing a report of research findings. Even if you don't carry out any primary research, this book is worthwhile because it will make you a more savvy consumer of the published research that you will need to consult for any project.

Van Maanen, J., Dabbs, J. M., & Faulkner, R. R. (1982). *Varieties of qualitative research.* Beverly Hills, CA: Sage.
This book is part of a six-volume series on *Studying Innovations in Methodology,* and by its title suggests that it offers some choices among nontraditional and nonreactive techniques and measures. If you would like to explore some alternative ways of gathering data—other than a questionnaire, for example—consider thumbing through this for some ideas.

Other business research methods books include:

Blank, S. C. (1984) *Practical business research methods.* Westport, CT: AVI Publishing.

Emory, W. (1985). *Business research methods.* Homewood, IL: Irwin.

CREATIVE PROBLEM-SOLVING SOURCES

Michalko, M. (1991). *Thinkertoys.* Berkeley, CA: Ten Speed.

That's thinkertoys, not Tinkertoys. This book is chock full of highly creative, some off-the-wall and others less radical, exercises and suggestions to boost the creative prowess of yourself and your group (and even your client). Stuck on identifying what the underlying problem is in your fieldwork case? Try "False Faces," which forces you to reverse your assumptions about the problem. A new approach to idea generation can be just the right medicine for avoiding groupthink or just plain ordinary thinking leading to yawn-producing solutions.

Van Gundy, A. B. (1992). *Idea power.* New York: AMACOM.

Another great source for group (and individual) creative-thinking techniques. In this volume, many chapters come complete with sample exercises for you to do with a clear series of steps to follow. These methods will benefit you far beyond your fieldwork assignment, helping you to think "out of the box."

GOVERNMENT AGENCIES

Here is a list of the field offices of the Small Business Administration, from the latest *U.S. Government Manual.*

REGION I

Office	*Address*	*Telephone*
Augusta, ME	Rm. 512, 40 Western Ave., 04330	207-662-8378
Boston, MA	9th Fl., 155 Federal St., 02110	617-451-2023
Boston, MA	Rm. 265, 10 Causeway St., 02222-1093	617-565-5590
Concord, NH	Rm. 210, 55 Pleasant St., 03302-1257	603-225-1400
Hartford, CT	2nd. Fl., 330 Main St., 06106	203-240-4700
Montpelier, VT	Rm. 205, 87 State St., 05602	802-828-4474
Providence, RI	380 Westminster Mall, 02903	401-528-4561
Springfield, MA	Rm. 212, 1550 Main St., 01103	413-785-9484

REGION II

Office	*Address*	*Telephone*
Buffalo, NY	Rm. 1311, 111 W. Huron St., 14202	716-846-4305
Camden, NJ	2600 Mt. Ephrain, 08104	609-757-4511
Elmira, NY	333 E. Water St., 14901	607-734-1571
Hato Rey, PR	Rm. 691, Federal Bldg., Carlos Charon Ave., 00918	809-766-5003

Melville, NY	Rm. 102E, 35 Pinelaw Rd., 11747	516-454-0764
New York, NY	Rm. 31-08, 26 Federal Plz., 10278	212-264-1450
Newark, NJ	4th Fl., 60 Park Pl., 07102	201-645-3580
Rochester, NY	Rm. 601, 100 State St., 14614	716-263-6700
St. Croix, VI	Rm. 7, United Shopping Plz., 4C&D State Sion Farm Christiansted, 00820	809-778-5380
St. Thomas, VI	Rm. 283, Federal Office Bldg., Veterans Dr., 00801	809-774-8530
Syracuse, NY	Rm. 1071, 100 S. Clinton St., 13260	315-423-5371

REGION III

Office	Address	Telephone
Baltimore, MD	3rd Fl., 10 N. Calvert St., 21202	301-962-2054
Charleston, WV	Rm. 309, 550 Eagan St., 25301	304-347-5220
Clarksburg, WV	5th Fl., 168 W. Main St., 26301	304-623-4317
Harrisburg, PA	Rm. 309, 100 Chestnut St., 17101	717-782-3846
King of Prussia, PA	Suite 201, 475 Allendale Rd., 19406	215-962-3710
Pittsburgh, PA	5th Fl., 960 Penn Ave., 15222	412-644-4306
Richmond, VA	Rm. 3015, 400 N. 5th St., 23240	804-771-2741
Washington, DC	6th Fl., 1111 18th St. NW., 20036	202-634-1805
Wilkes-Barre, PA	Rm. 2327, 20 N. Pennsylvania Ave., 18701	717-826-6446
Wilmington, DE	Rm. 412, 920 N. King St., 19801	302-573-6295

REGION IV

Office	Address	Telephone
Atlanta, GA	5th Fl., 1375 Peachtree St. NE, 30367	404-347-4999
Atlanta, GA	6th Fl., 1720 Peachtree St. NW, 30309	404-347-4749
Birmingham, AL	Suite 200, 2121 8th Ave. N., 35203	205-731-1341
Charlotte, NC	200 N. College St., 28202	704-371-6561
Columbia, SC	Rm. 358, 1835 Assembly St., 29202	803-253-5339
181 Coral Gables, FL	Suite 501, 1320 S. Dixie Hwy., 33136	305-536-5533
Gulfport, MS	Suite 1001, 1 Hancock Plz., 39501	601-863-4449
Jackson, MS	Suite 322, 101 W. Capitol St., 39269	601-965-4363
Jacksonville, FL	Suite 100B, 7825 Bay Meadows Way, 32202	904-443-1900
Louisville, KY	Rm. 188, 600 M. L. King, Jr., Pl. 40202	502-582-5976
Nashville, TN	Suite 201, 50 Vantage Way, 37228	615-736-5850
Statesboro, GA	Rm. 225, 52 N. Main St., 30458	912-489-8719
Tampa, FL	Rm. 104, 501 E. Polk St., 33602-3945	813-228-2594
West Palm Beach, FL	Suite 402, 2601 Corporate Way, 33407	305-689-3922

REGION V

Office	Address	Telephone
Chicago, IL	Rm. 1975, 300 S. Riverside Plz., 60606-6611	312-353-0359
Chicago, IL	Rm. 1250, 500 W. Madison St., 60661	312-353-4528
Cincinnati, OH	Suite 870, 525 Vine St., 45202	513-684-2814
Cleveland, OH	Rm. 317, 1240 E. 9th St., 44199	216-522-4180
Columbus, OH	Rm. 512, 85 Marconi Blvd., 43215	614-469-7310
Detroit, MI	Rm. 515, 477 Michigan Ave., 48226	313-226-7240
Indianapolis, IN	Suite 100, 429 N. Pennsylvania St., 46204-1873	317-226-7275
Madison, WI	Rm. 213, 212 E. Washington Ave., 53703	608-264-5268
Marquette, MI	300 S. Front St.	906-225-1108
Milwaukee, WI	Suite 400, 310 W. Wisconsin Ave., 53203	414-291-1094
Minneapolis, MN	610-C Butler Sq., 100 N. 6th St., 55403	612-370-2306
Springfield, IL	Suite 302, 511 W. Capitol St., 62704	217-492-4232

REGION VI

Office	Address	Telephone
Albuquerque, NM	Suite 320, 625 Silver Ave. SW, 87102	505-262-6339
Austin, TX	Rm. 520, 300 E. 8th St., 78701	512-482-5288
Corpus Christi, TX	Suite 1200, 606 N. Carancahua, 78476	512-888-3301
Dallas, TX	Bldg. C, 8625 King George Dr., 75235	214-767-7611
Dallas, TX	Rm. 3C-36, 1100 Commerce St., 45242	214-767-0600
El Paso, TX	Suite 320, 10737 Gateway W., 79935	915-540-5676
Fort Worth, TX	Rm. 10A27, 819 Taylor St., 76102	817-334-3673
Harlingen, TX	Suite 500, 222 E. Van Buren, 78550	512-427-8533
Houston, TX	Suite 112, 2525 Murworth St., 77054	713-660-4401
Little Rock, AR	Suite 601, 320 W. Capitol Ave., 72201	501-378-5277
Lubbock, TX	Suite 200, 1611 10th St., 79401	806-743-7462
Marshall, TX	Rm. 103, 505 E. Travis St., 75670	214-935-5257
New Orleans, LA	Suite 2000, 1661 Canal St., 70112	504-589-2744
Oklahoma City, OK	Suite 670, 200 NW 5th St., 73102	405-231-5237
San Antonio, TX	Suite 200, 7400 Blanco Rd., 78216	512-229-4501
Shreveport, LA	Rm. 8A-08, 500 Fannin St., 71101	318-226-5196

REGION VII

Office	Address	Telephone
Cedar Rapids, IA	Rm. 100, 373 Collins Rd. NE., 52404	319-399-2571
Des Moines, IA	Rm. 749, 210 Walnut St., 50309	515-284-4567
Kansas City, MO	13th Fl., 911 Walnut St., 64106	816-426-3316
Kansas City, MO	Suite 501, 323 W. 8th St., 64106	816-374-6760

Omaha, NE	11145 Mill Valley Rd., 68154	402-221-3620
Springfield, MO	Suite 110, 620 S. Glenstone St., 65802	417-864-7670
St. Louis, MO	Rm. 242, 815 Olive St., 63101	314-539-6600
Wichita, KS	1st Fl., 110 E. Waterman St., 67202	316-269-6566

REGION VIII

Office	*Address*	*Telephone*
Casper, WY	Rm. 4001, 100 East B St., 82602	307-261-5761
Denver, CO	Suite 701, 999 18th St., 80202	303-294-7021
Denver, CO	Rm. 407, 721 19th St., 80201	303-844-6501
Fargo, ND	Rm. 218, 657 2d Ave. N., 58108	701-239-5131
Helena, MT	Rm. 528, 301 S. Park, 59626	406-449-5381
Salt Lake City, UT	Rm. 2237, 125 S. State St., 84138	801-524-5804
Sioux Falls, SD	Suite 101, 101 S. Main Ave., 57102	605-330-4231

REGION IX

Office	*Address*	*Telephone*
Agana, GU	Rm. 508, 238 Archbishop F.C. Flores St., 96910	671-472-7277
Fresno, CA	2719 N. Air Fresno Dr., 93727	209-487-5791
Honolulu, HI	Rm. 2213, 300 Ala Moana, 96850	808-541-2990
Las Vegas, NV	301 E. Stewart, 89125	702-388-6611
Los Angeles, CA	Suite 1200, 330 N. Brand Blvd., Glendale, 91203	213-894-2977
Phoenix, AZ	5th Fl., 2005 N. Central Ave., 85004	602-379-3737
Reno, NV	P.O. Box 3216, Rm. 238, 50 S. Virginia St., 89505	702-784-5268
Sacramento, CA	Suite 215, 660 J St., 95814	916-551-1445
San Diego, CA	Suite 4-S-29, 880 Front St., 92188	619-557-7252
San Francisco, CA	20th Fl., 71 Stevenson St., 94105	415-774-6402
San Francisco, CA	4th Fl., 211 Main St., 94105	415-744-6801
Santa Ana, CA	Rm. 160, 901 W. Civic Center Dr.	714-836-2494
Tucson, AZ	Rm. 3V, 300 W. Congress St., 85701	602-629-6715
Ventura, CA	Suite 10, Bldg. C-1, 6477 Telephone Rd., 93003	805-642-1866

REGION X

Office	*Address*	*Telephone*
Anchorage, AK	Rm. A36, No. 67, 222 W. 8th Ave., 99501	907-271-4022

Boise, ID	Suite 290, 1020 Main St., 83702	208-334-9641
Portland, OR	Suite 500, 220 SW Columbia St., 97204	503-326-5221
Seattle, WA	Rm. 400, 2615 4th Ave., 98121	206-553-5534
Seattle, WA	Rm. 1792, 915 2nd. Ave., 98174	206-553-2786
Spokane, WA	10th Fl. E., W. 601 1st Ave., 99210	509-353-2807

PERIODICALS

Media 3 Publications, *Atlanta Small Business Monthly* (monthly), 1853 D, Peeler Road, Atlanta GA 30338, 404-394-2811.

Gives practical information for owners of small to mid-sized businesses. Topics covered include advertising, marketing, finance management, selling, and customer service.

Commerce Clearing House, Inc., *Business Franchise Guide* (two basic volumes plus monthly reports), 4025 W. Peterson Ave., Chicago IL 60646, 312-583-8500.

Dun & Bradstreet Credit Services, *D & B Reports* (bi-monthly), Murray Hill, NJ.

Contains articles and feature reports on the economy, economic indicators, office technology, Washington, D.C., taxes, export/import, and sales/marketing. Contains a newsletter called *Dun & Bradstreet Looks at Business* that includes current statistics on business expectations, business starts, business failures, and other information relevant to small business.

Entrepreneur Inc., *Entrepreneur* (monthly), 2392 Morse Ave., Irvine, CA 92714, 714-261-2325.

Provides information on small business operation.

Entrepreneur Inc., *Entrepreneurial Woman* (monthly), 2392 Morse Ave., Irvine, CA 92714, 714-261-2325.

Provides information for women on opening and operating a business.

Baylor University, Hankamer School of Business, *Entrepreneurship: Theory and Practice* (quarterly), John F. Baugh Center for Entrepreneurship, BU Box 98011, Waco, TX 76798-8011, 817-755-2265.

Formerly published as the *American Journal of Small Business;* publishes articles in all areas of entrepreneurship, small business, and family business. United States Association for Small Business and Entrepreneurship official journal.

Goldhirsh Group, Inc., *INC.: The Magazine for Growing Companies* (monthly), 38 Commercial Wharf, Boston, MA 02110, 617-248-8000.

Profiles of companies, stories of successful entrepreneurs, and articles covering a wide range of topics of interest to growing companies are included in each issue. Contains annual features such as "The Most Entrepreneurial Cities in the U.S."

Jossey-Bass Inc., *Family Business Review* (quarterly), 350 Sansome St., 5th Fl., San Francisco, CA 94104, 415-433-1767.
The latest ideas and strategies for professionals and scholars who work with family businesses.

West Virginia University, Bureau of Business Research, *Journal of Small Business Management* (quarterly), Box 6025, Morgantown, WV 26506-6025, 304-293-7534.
Each issue contains articles, features, and editorials on small business management and entrepreneurship. A bibliographic "Resources" section and book reviews are included.

Minnesota Ventures Inc., *Minnesota Ventures* (bi-monthly), 10 S. Fifth St., No. 415, Minneapolis, MN 55402, 612-338-3828.
Provides practical information for small to mid-sized companies.

Success Services Australasia Pty., Ltd., *Success Magazine* (bi-monthly), 505 St. Kilda Rd., Melbourne, Vic. 3004, Australia, 613-876-2000.
Covers changing philosophies and techniques in business.

NEWSLETTERS

American Small Business Association, *A.S.B.D. Today* (bi-monthly), 1800 N. Kent St., Suite 910, Arlington, VA 76051, 800-235-3298.

Research Done Right, *Bootstrappin' Entrepreneur; The Newsletter for Individuals With Great Ideas and a Little Bit of Cash* (quarterly), 8726 S. Sepulveda Blvd., Suite B261-UI, Los Angeles, CA 90045, 310-568-9861.
Newsletter concerned with starting and building businesses on small budgets. Areas covered include low-cost marketing strategies, management ideas, and success stories.

Irongate Graphics, *Home-Run Business Newsletter* (bi-monthly), 7627 Iron Gate Ln., Frederick, MD 21702, 301-473-4393.

Index

Action plan, 49-52
Alternatives:
    evaluation of, 105-107
    generation of, 104-105
    selection of, 107-108
Annotated Bibliography (Appendix C),
    123-134
    business plans, 124-126
    demographics, 124
    entrepreneurship and small business,
    124-126
    industry classification, 124
    industry surveys, 124-125
    international entrepreneurship, 126
    manufacturers information, 124
    new ventures, 124-126
    small business sources, 126
    venture capital, 125
    women-owned businesses, 125
Assessment phase, 30

Business information sources, 89

Client:
    best, 22
    communication, 60
    determining needs of, 40-46
    evaluation by student team, 59
    evaluation of fieldwork, 10-11
    initial meeting, 37-40

    second meeting, 40
Confidentiality, 115-117
Conflict:
    group, 80
    role, 80

Deliverables, presentation to client, 42-46

Environment:
    client firm, 34-36
    general, 31-33
    industry, 33-34
Establishing objectives, 46-48
Establishing business contacts, 8-9
Ethical considerations, (Appendix A),
    115-117

Fieldwork:
    appropriate, 18-19
    comparison to textbook cases, 2-3
    contribution to education, 4-5
    myths about, 21-28
    preparing yourself, 13-15
    reasons for participating in, 5-9
    role of students, 9-10
    role of university/college, 12-13
    typical projects, 20-21
Final report, 54-56
Follow-up activities, 59-61

Group (*see also* Team):
    discussion, 58-59
    dynamics, 77-79
    formation, 73-77
    structure, 68-73
    versus working alone, 23

Implementation phase, 46-48, 108-111
Information:
    gathering, 31-36, 89-94
    interpreting, 95-97
    interviews, 92-94
    organizing, 94-95
    primary sources, 87, 90-94
    sample survey, 91
    secondary sources, 87,89, 123-134
    surveys and questionnaires, 90-92
Interviews, 92-94
Intuition, 97

Killer phrases, 88

Mindguarding, 96

Nonreactive methods, 93-94
Number-crunching, 97

Oral presentation, 57-58

Plan execution, 52-54
Practical experience, 5-6
Preliminary analyses, 36-37
Professionalism (Appendix A), 115-117

Project, purpose of, 40-46
Project manager, 68-70

Results phase, 56-59

Small Business Administration, 14
    role of in fieldwork (Appendix B),
    119-122
Small Business Institute, 14
    role of in fieldwork (Appendix B),
    119-122
Surveys, 90-92

Task managers, 70
Teams:
    communication, 74-76
    comedian, 72
    computer/statistics whiz, 72
    cross-disciplinary, 66
    decision-making, 75-76
    evaluation, 59-60
    externally-focused, 67
    grunt, 72
    members, 70-73
    motivation, 76-77
    nature of, 64-67
    problems, 81-82
    productivity, 77
    roles, 70-73
    spokesperson, 72
    trust and cooperation, 78-79
    writer/editor, 72
Technical writing, 111-112
Textbook cases, 2-3
Timelines and deadlines, 50-52

About the Authors

Lisa K. Gundry, Ph.D., is Associate Professor of Management in the College of Commerce at DePaul University. She teaches courses in Entrepreneurship, Organizational Behavior, and Creativity in Business. She has published many research articles in journals including *Organizational Dynamics, Human Relations, Family Business Review, IEEE Transactions on Engineering Management, Journal of Management Education (Organizational Behavior Teaching Review),* and *Journal of Business and Psychology.* Her research interests include entrepreneurial management, creativity and innovation, organizational culture, and cross-cultural entrepreneurship. She received her Ph.D. from Northwestern University, and in 1994 received the Quality of Instruction Council's award for Excellence in Teaching at DePaul University.

Aaron A. Buchko, Ph.D., is Associate Professor of Management in the College of Business, Bradley University, teaching graduate and undergraduate courses in Planning and Strategy and a graduate course in Executive Development. Prior to entering the academic field, he worked for several years in production, sales, and marketing, and was the senior marketing officer for a publishing company. He attended Michigan State University and earned his Ph.D. in Management, with an emphasis on corporate strategy. His research and writing focuses on planning and competitive strategy, and he has published more than twenty articles in various academic journals and professional publications, including the *Academy of Management Journal* and *Advances in Strategic Management.*

He is a confidential advisor to executives in many organizations, primarily in the areas of planning, strategy, and executive development. In addition, he conducts numerous professional seminars yearly for several corporations and is a frequent speaker to trade and civic associations on the topics of competition and strategy. In 1992, he received Bradley University's New Faculty Achievement Award for Teaching.

CPSIA information can be obtained at www.ICGtesting.com
Printed in the USA
BVOW07s1547231114

376362BV00001B/3/A

9 780803 972018